YOUR YEAR-RO
INVESTMENT PLANN

NANCY DUNNAN

I0642544

PERENNIAL LIBRARY

HARPER & ROW, PUBLISHERS
New York
Cambridge
Philadelphia
San Francisco
Washington
London
Mexico City
São Paulo
Singapore
Sydney

I wish to thank the following people, who provided the most valuable ingredient in the world of investing, information.

Betsy Flager, Merrill Lynch, New York
Ellen Flaherty, E. F. Research Associates, Williamsport, PA
Christine W. Hsu, Seidman & Seidman, New York
Kenneth S. Janke, National Association of Investment Clubs, Royal Oak, MI
Barry Levine, E. F. Hutton, New York
Gregory D. Murphy, E. F. Hutton, New York
Jay J. Pack, Silberberg Rosenthal & Co., New York
Howard Rosenberg, Farkouh, Furman & Faccio, New York
The research staff at Dean Witter, New York

Special appreciation to Helen Moore, my editor at Harper & Row and the initiator of this book, and Kathy Hom, my assistant.

YOUR YEAR-ROUND INVESTMENT PLANNER. Copyright © 1988 by Harper & Row, Publishers, Inc. All rights reserved. Printed in the United States of America. No part of this book may be used or reproduced in any manner whatsoever without written permission except in the case of brief quotations embodied in critical articles and reviews. For information address Harper & Row, Publishers, Inc., 10 East 53rd Street, New York, N.Y. 10022. Published simultaneously in Canada by Fitzhenry & Whiteside Limited, Toronto.

FIRST EDITION

Library of Congress Cataloging-in-Publication Data

Dunnan, Nancy.
  Your year-round investment planner.

  1. Investments—Handbooks, manuals, etc.   I. Title.
HG4527.D777 1988   332.6'78   87-25848
ISBN 0-06-096245-3 (pbk.)

88 89 90 91 92 RRD 10 9 8 7 6 5 4 3 2 1

CONTENTS

INTRODUCTION

Living well is the best revenge.

—George Herbert

How you choose to live well may be quite different from the way your neighbor, your colleague, or your sister chooses. But regardless of the life-style you favor, you'll live well if you also invest well. In the 1980s living well means having money, handling it wisely, and knowing how to make it work best for you.

The easy life of forever skiing in St. Moritz, surfing off Santa Barbara, or picking blueberries in Vermont is a dream for most of us, except for that blissful two-week vacation. With the soaring cost of living, I suspect that the only people who can afford to travel with the seasons today either live off their daddy's credit card or manage their own money with great effectiveness.

Getting started, of course, is always the hardest part. The complexity of today's financial world provides us all with a plausible excuse for inaction. We can easily talk ourselves out of doing something and into doing nothing because there are simply too many choices. How can you decide whether to invest in a REIT, a RELP, or a JUNK? Who's to say which is best, an EE, a CD, or a Zero? In fact, what ever happened to blue chips and utility stocks?

If those are your excuses, you can forget them now. We've taken the mystery out of investing and replaced it with an intelligent, common-sense view of money management. By the time you finish *Your Year-Round Investment Planner,* not only will you be playing hardball on Wall Street, you'll also be playing softball at your country house whenever the whim strikes.

HOW TO USE THIS BOOK

Wondering what to do with the 100 shares of Clorox you inherited? Forgotten what you paid for IBM 5 years ago? Uncertain when that 9% CD comes due? Thinking about buying a new mutual fund or getting in on the gold stampede?

Savvy handling of these and other everyday financial issues is the key to making money work for you, to becoming financially secure. In order to head down the path to riches you don't need to comprehend every detail in the 1986 Tax Reform Act. Nor do you need to memorize the symbols for the stocks listed on the New York Stock Exchange. In fact, effective control of money is far easier than most people realize. It's based on two very simple concepts: one, being organized, and two, being well informed. *Your Year-Round Investment Planner* addresses these two points, showing you exactly how to keep track of your money and how to know which investments are best for you—today, tomorrow, and 10 years from now.

Your planner covers the money basics we all worry about:

- What interest you're getting on your money market fund
- What tax bracket you're in and what to do about it
- What you can expect from social security
- What you should do with your IRA
- Whether your stocks have gone up or down in price
- Whether you should refinance your mortgage
- Whether you should sign up for a dividend reinvestment plan

Your planner is divided into six sections. Part 1, Getting Started, focuses on you and your financial life, what it's like now and what you'd like it to be like next year, in 5 years, in 10. You'll learn to build on your strengths, set benchmarks for yourself, and find ways to reach them. In this section you'll also get your house in order, organize those papers, and list the people who play an important role in your money world.

Part 2, Tracking Your Investments, describes the top 20 types of investments in an easy-to-understand manner. They are arranged by level of safety, with the safest investments presented first. These investments run the gamut, from EE savings bonds and your bank account to precious metals and limited partnerships. You'll learn the pros and cons of each, and whether they're right for you. Opposite each one is a worksheet tailored to that particular investment. If you decide on a purchase, you'll be able to chart its progress directly on the worksheet so that you can clearly determine at any time whether you're making or losing money, and at what speed.

Part 3, Through the Financial Maze, explains how to find and manage a stockbroker, a banker, and a mutual fund. No longer will you be bamboozled by complicated monthly statements or hard-to-follow reports. It's all explained in this section.

Part 4, Taxing Issues, discusses the 1986 Tax Reform Act, what it is and how it impacts on your investments. Our specially designed Tax Checklist contains a thumbnail sketch of more than a dozen easy ways to pay Uncle Sam less and yourself more.

Part 5, Retirement Planning, emphasizes the importance of planning to make your golden years happy, worry-free ones. You'll learn to evaluate retirement plans from company pensions to salary reduction plans like 401(k)s, so you can study your options and make intelligent decisions about future investments.

Part 6, Your Financial Calendar, contains one blank page for each of the 12 months, where you can keep track of all your financial activities. Advice is provided to help you get started. Never again will you forget a CD coming due, fail to file a tax form, or miss lunch with your broker.

This book offers only general investment observations based on the author's experience and makes no specific recommendations.

It is intended and written to provide the author's opinions in regard to the subject matter covered. The author and the publisher are not engaged in rendering legal, accounting, or other professional advice and the reader should seek the services of a qualified professional for such advice.

The author and the publisher cannot be held responsible for any loss incurred as a result of the application of any of the information in this publication.

PART ONE

GETTING STARTED

Everyone, even a 10-year-old child, knows that before you make a batch of cookies you must line up all the ingredients, otherwise you'll never have an opportunity to taste those yummy fudge brownies or luscious lemon squares. So too with making money. If you're really serious about building your wealth, you must begin by lining up all the ingredients in your personal portfolio. The pros call this determining your *net worth*—the sum total of what you own (your assets) minus what you owe (your liabilities).

In other words, your net worth is what would be left over if you cashed in all your assets and paid off all your debts.

Once you know the score, making smart money decisions is much easier. You'll know what ingredients to add or subtract from your personal recipe for financial success.

Calculating your net worth will probably yield a pleasant surprise: most of us are worth far more than we think. If you're skeptical, if you think you're not worth much, or that this is an exercise in futility dreamed up by financial planners with nothing better to do, think again. Do you own a car? A sapphire ring or a pair of gold cufflinks? Have you stashed away those savings bonds you received for graduation? Do you have a money market account or shares in a mutual fund? If so, you're well on your way to chalking up a respectable net worth.

Your net worth is the ultimate measure of your financial progress. It's your personal Dow Jones Industrial Average, and it's best to take this inventory at least once a year, say on January 1, April Fool's Day, or your birthday. Then, by comparing your net worth from one year to the next you'll know exactly how rapidly you're becoming a millionaire!

KNOWING WHAT YOU'RE WORTH

STEP 1   The simplest way to take inventory is to set up a balance sheet like the one below. Plan on spending 2 to 3 hours on this, plus time for several phone calls. List your assets on the left and your liabilities on the right. *Liquid assets*, those that can readily be converted into cash, include your bank accounts, money market mutual funds, stocks, bonds, and other investments. List these at their current market value, or what you would receive for them today if you sold them, and not at the price you originally paid. *Nonliquid assets* are more difficult to evaluate. If, for example, you've invested in a limited partnership, you will have to list the amount you paid since these have a very inactive secondary market. *Fixed assets* include your house and any other real estate, your car, and all personal possessions.

STEP 2   After you've tallied up what you own, itemize your liabilities, or what you owe. *Short-term liabilities* are obligations that must be paid off within a year. For example, if your car loan has 8 months to go, it falls into this category, as do credit card balances and other bills. *Long-term debt* refers to the balance due on your mortgage and other loans due in a year or more.

THE BENEFITS

The advantages of calculating your net worth are many: (1) it's easier to determine if you're carrying sufficient homeowners or rental insurance; (2) you have an instant snapshot of your financial strengths and weaknesses; (3) your debt-to-asset ratio is crystal clear; (4) you know whether your investments are on target; (5) the danger spots are immediately obvious—if, for example, you don't feel as rich as you look on paper, it could be that too much of your net worth is tied up in tangibles (like cars or jewelry) that aren't generating a positive cash flow. Or perhaps you've never taken time to draw up serious financial goals.

FINDING YOUR NET WORTH

Date _____

ASSETS

Cash on hand	$_____
Cash in checking accounts	_____
Savings accounts, money market fund	_____
Life insurance, cash value	_____
Annuities	_____
Retirement funds:	
IRA or Keogh	_____
401(k) Plan	_____
Vested interest in pension or profit-sharing plan	_____
U.S. savings bonds, current value	_____
Investments:	
Market value of stocks, bonds, mutual fund shares, etc.	_____
Real estate, market value of real property minus mortgage	_____
Property:	
Automobile	_____
Furniture	_____
Jewelry, furs	_____
Sports and hobby equipment	_____
Equity interest in your business	_____
Total assets:	$_____

Date _____

LIABILITIES

Unpaid bills:	
Charge accounts	$_____
Taxes, property taxes, and quarterly income taxes	_____
Insurance premiums	_____
Rent or monthly mortgage payment	_____
Utilities	_____
Balance due on:	
Mortgage	_____
Automobile loans	_____
Personal loans	_____
Installment loans	_____
Total liabilities	$_____

Assets	$_____
Minus liabilities	_____
Your net worth:	$_____

SETTING FINANCIAL GOALS

YOUR INVENTORY TELLS ALL

Now that you've drawn up your personal balance sheet, you'll find it easier to take stock of your financial situation, something most of us tend to avoid doing. Indeed, there's no more hiding from the facts: if you're in debt it shows; on the other hand, if you're making money, that too is clearly spelled out. Here are three key points you should look for in your net worth statement.

ASSET MIX   Review your list of assets. If you have a $5,000 CD, a $9,000 mink coat with matching hat and muff, 100 shares of IBM, and a $30,000 Jaguar, clearly you're involved with immediate gratification and are spending too much on "things." You hardly need be told that you should increase your cash savings as well as your holdings in stocks, bonds, and even real estate, in order to build income-generating assets.

DIVERSIFICATION   It's obviously poor financial planning to put all your eggs in one basket, so if most of your funds are invested in your company's stock ownership plan, in real estate, or any other one security, take immediate steps to diversify. Your company could fall on hard times. The market could drop. Real estate values could plummet. The ideal mix, of course, depends on your age, income level, and attitude toward risk.

LIQUID HOLDINGS   This category should constitute 20 to 40% (even 50% if you're very conservative or retired) of your total assets. These funds, at a minimum, should be adequate to cover 3 months of living expenses. In addition, you need cash for emergencies as well as for making investments as opportunities arise.

GETTING DOWN TO IT

We all like to think of ourselves as age 24 and holding, but like me, you may have been holding for some time now. Life has a way of marching by very quickly: before you know it you're attending your fifth college reunion, the house is too small, the kids are ready for college, or you're just a few years away from retirement.

That's why goals are crucial, no matter how old you are, for without them it's almost impossible to control your financial destiny. Personal goals are rather like your company's 1-, 5-, and 10-year game plans: they chart progress, give you something tangible to aim for, and prevent heedless spending on pie in the sky.

You don't need a Ph.D. in economics to establish your goals, but you do need to be serious about your financial well-being. Begin by writing down everything you'd like to accomplish. Don't worry about the order or whether your list seems silly or extravagant. Then, relist the items in order of importance: owning a house may be more important than buying a yacht that sleeps six; or establishing a nest egg may take precedence over having a Saab 1800 in the garage. Next, divide your list into short-term goals (those you can achieve in a year or less) and long-term (those that take over a year to accomplish). Use the worksheet on page 12 for this purpose.

Once you have listed your goals in order of priority and determined whether you need more or less than a year to meet them, assign each one a rough dollar amount. It's important to commit both the goal and the cost to paper. Then you can determine how much you need to set aside on an annual, monthly, or even weekly basis. If you find it difficult to save, arrange with your bank to have the amount deposited directly from your paycheck or from your checking account into a money market account. From there you can redirect it to the appropriate investment.

If you are married or have children, some of your goals will automatically involve your family. Your chances of achieving your goals are, of course, far greater if your family agrees with them. Share your list with your husband, wife, consort, or children. Ask for ideas. Work together. If financing college education is top priority, for instance, discuss it with your children. This will not only instill financial responsibility, it will make them aware of what school costs, what expenses you expect them to cover, and what your values are.

Your goals, along with your net worth, will continually change. And, as you take pleasure in crossing off one goal from your master list, you can plan for the future by adding yet another. You'll find it becomes more fun as the years go by, and before you know it, those seemingly frivolous goals of 5 years ago—to buy a motorcycle or live in a houseboat—are now at the top of the list!

IMPORTANT PAPERS AND PEOPLE

Whenever you need a critical document, such as a stock certificate, a will, or an insurance policy, it's guaranteed to be somewhat of an emergency. You almost always need these papers in a hurry, but most of us never know precisely where they are. (They're not the type of thing you read on lazy Sunday afternoons.) So, to help you avoid scurrying through desk drawers and musty trunks in the attic, we've devised an organizational tracking system for all your key financial papers. If you take time now to fill in the worksheets that follow, you and your family, like the Boy Scouts, will always *be prepared.*

You may want to make two copies of certain documents, keeping one at home and one in your safe-deposit box or with your lawyer. Some documents you keep forever; others have a limited shelf life. Those that fall into the safe-deposit-box category are almost always kept permanently.

Copies of these lists should be given to key people—your spouse, lawyer, executor, and one of your adult children.

An up-to-date household inventory is critical in the event of fire or theft. Most people, when asked by their insurance agent to list their possessions, are able to recall from memory only about half of them. In order to obtain adequate refunds from your insurance company, you need not only a list of your worldly goods but also receipts and appraisals to document their original prices and current value. It's best to videotape or take photos of your home and possessions. (Check with your insurance agent for the name of a reliable video photographer; most charge by the hour.) Make at least two copies, one for your insurance agent, the other for your safe-deposit box. (Don't leave it at home; it might burn in the fire.)

What you need to keep track of is the name of each item, its location, the purchase price, when and where it was purchased, and the location of any warranty and receipt. Consider purchasing a photo album and recording all this information on the back of the photograph of each item.

SAFE DEPOSIT BOX RECORD

Name of bank:

Contact:

Address & telephone:

Box number:

Opened: Annual fee: $

Names & telephones of people with keys:

IMPORTANT PAPERS

FILED IN SAFE-DEPOSIT BOX	POLICY/ CERT. NO.	COMPANY/ INSTITUTION
Adoption papers	_____	_____
Automobile titles	_____	_____
Birth certificate	_____	_____
Bonds	_____	_____
Citizenship papers	_____	_____
Divorce papers	_____	_____
Household inventory	_____	_____
Marriage documents	_____	_____
Military papers	_____	_____
Passport	_____	_____
Real estate deeds	_____	_____
Stock certificates	_____	_____
Will	_____	_____
FILED AT HOME		
Annuities	_____	_____
Auto insurance policy	_____	_____
Bankbooks & monthly statements	_____	_____
Credit card list	_____	_____
Educational records	_____	_____
Federal tax returns	_____	_____
Homeowners insurance policy	_____	_____
Household inventory & appraisals (copy with insurance agent)	_____	_____
Income tax returns	_____	_____
IRA records	_____	_____
Life insurance policy	_____	_____
List of advisors	_____	_____
Medical insurance policy	_____	_____
Pension plan records	_____	_____
Real estate taxes	_____	_____
Social security records	_____	_____
Will	_____	_____

YOUR ADVISORS

Use the space below as your personal directory of financial advisors. Gather this information before you need it. Consider using the margins to note the best time of day to reach each advisor.

YOUR ADVISOR'S NAME   ADDRESS   TELEPHONE

Accountant:

_____   _____   _____

Attorney:

_____   _____   _____

Banker:

_____   _____   _____

Estate executor:

_____   _____   _____

Insurance agents:

Auto _____   _____   _____

House _____   _____   _____

Life _____   _____   _____

Medical _____   _____   _____

Disability _____   _____   _____

Other _____   _____   _____

Stockbroker:

_____   _____   _____

Tax advisor:

_____   _____   _____

Trustee of children's account:

_____   _____   _____

Trust officer:

_____   _____   _____

YOUR FINANCIAL GOALS

Take pride in crossing off the goals you've met and take pleasure in adding new ones.

GOAL	DATE SET	NUMBER OF YEARS TO REACH	TOTAL $ NEEDED	$ ON HAND	SAVE MONTHLY	INVESTMENT CHOICES

PART TWO

TRACKING YOUR INVESTMENTS

This section contains the essential facts about the 20 leading investments, some of which you may already have in your portfolio. Read them carefully to determine which ones are clearly best for you, which will help you achieve your goals, and which will not. Then, photocopy the worksheets for your choices—make several copies if you need extra space—and begin filling them in. Try to set aside one morning a month to do your paperwork. You'll find it's an effortless way to monitor your portfolio. By keeping your worksheets up to date, you'll always be in command of your money, know exactly when to sell a losing investment, when to buy more of a winner, and when to sit still and tally up the profits!

U.S. SAVINGS BONDS

Series EE savings bonds, sold by the U.S. government to individual investors, are one of the least expensive and safest ways to save money. Yet Americans often overlook this totally secure investment in their quest for a more glamorous road to riches, primarily because, until 1982, EE bonds offered pitifully low yields. Rates today, which are tied to the Treasury-bill rate (see U.S. Treasury Issues) are far more competitive. The current minimum for bonds held 5 years is 6%. But if the 5-year T-bill rate is higher than 6%, the bonds will pay the higher rate—85% of the T-bill market average. Since when inflation rises, interest rates usually move up also, this variable rate is a distinct advantage. And with the current minimum at 6%, you will double your money in 12 years, risk-free.

BEST FOR

- Conservative and/or small investors.
- Those planning to meet a financial goal several years from now.
- Children's accounts.
- Those seeking a financial gift that's easy to give and will grow in value.

MINIMUM INVESTMENT

- These bonds sell at a discount from face value, which means a $50 bond actually costs only $25; a $100 bond is $50.
- They come in a variety of denominations: $50, $75, $100, $200, $500, $1,000, $5,000 and $10,000.
- You may purchase only $30,000 in face value (for $15,000) in any one calendar year.

PROS

- Backed by the full faith and credit of the U.S. government.
- Rates generally higher than money market accounts and passbook savings.
- The interest rate, adjusted every 6 months (in May and November), is equal to 85% of the average 5-year T-bill rate.
- Bonds held less than 5 years earn interest at fixed, graduated rates, currently beginning at 4.16% and moving up to 6% for those held 5 years.
- There's no cap on how high the rate can go.
- Bonds are replaced free of charge if lost or stolen.

CONS

- Both principal and interest are tied up, because these bonds do not pay current interest; instead,

you buy them at a discount—half their face value—and redeem them at full face value. The face or redemption value minus the price you pay constitutes the interest.
- Not redeemable during the first 6 months.
- You must hold your bonds 5 years to receive the guaranteed minimum yield.
- With the rate at 6%, bonds mature in 12 years. (Savings bonds maturities are based on the time it takes a bond to increase in value from its issue price to its face amount at the minimum rate when purchased.)

WHERE TO BUY

- Commercial banks, savings & loans, Federal Reserve Banks directly, or through automatic payroll savings plans.

FEES

- None.

RISK LEVEL

- Very low; the safest type of investment available.

TAX IMPLICATIONS

- No state or local income taxes on interest earned; federal tax may be deferred until they are cashed in or mature.

KEEP IN MIND

- EE bonds are ideal for retirement. First, purchase bonds that will mature when you turn 65. Then you can roll them over into HH bonds, which provide interest payments twice a year and allow you to defer federal income tax on the interest until the HH bonds are cashed in or mature—in 10 years.
- Use EE bonds to accumulate money for your child's education and avoid the new "kiddie" tax. Buy bonds that will come due after your child turns 14 and put them in his or her name. Then the deferred tax, when due, will be taxed at the child's lower rate.
- For current interest rate, call: 1-800-US-BONDS; in Washington, DC: USA-8888.

YOUR INVESTMENT PLANNER FOR SERIES EE SAVINGS BONDS

Series EE bonds purchased between November 1982 and October 1986 pay a guaranteed minimum of 7½% interest if you keep the bonds for 5 years. Savings bonds purchased since November 1, 1986, pay a guaranteed minimum of 6%, again if held for 5 years. The government is free to change the guaranteed minimum at any time. Be sure to make a note here if the minimum guaranteed rate changes.

SERIES	BOND NUMBER	DATE PURCHASED	PURCHASE PRICE	FACE VALUE	NUMBER PURCHASED	TOTAL COST

Where certificates held:

Name certificates registered in:

Co-owner (if any):

U.S. TREASURY ISSUES

Backed by Uncle Sam, Treasury notes, bills, and bonds are as safe as savings bonds, although higher rates are available elsewhere—what you sacrifice in return you make up in safety. They are exempt from state and local, but not federal, taxes.

Treasury notes mature in 1 to 10 years. They pay a fixed interest rate twice a year, called the coupon rate. This rate is related to the note's length of maturity—the longer the maturity the higher the rate.

Treasury bills, or *T-bills,* mature in 13, 26, or 52 weeks and are the most short-term issues sold by the U.S. Treasury. They have no stated interest rate but instead are sold at a discount, that is, below face value. You receive that full face amount when the bill comes due, so, as with EE savings bonds, the difference between what you pay for the bill and what you receive upon maturity is basically the interest.

Treasury bonds are essentially the same as Treasury notes, except bonds are more long-term—they mature in 10 years or more, with 30 years generally being the longest possible maturity. As with T-notes, interest is paid twice a year.

BEST FOR

NOTES
- Small and/or conservative investors who want guaranteed interest income.
- Those who live in high income tax states.

T-BILLS
- Temporarily parking money in a safe place until investing it elsewhere.
- Transferring lump sums of money from one tax year to the next.

BONDS
- Investors seeking high yields with ultimate safety.
- As a long-term substitute for a money market fund.

MINIMUM INVESTMENT

NOTES
- $1,000 for notes that mature in 4 years or more.
- $5,000 for notes that mature in less than 4 years.

T-BILLS
- $10,000 with $5,000 increments.

BONDS
- $1,000.

PROS

- Principal and interest guaranteed by the full faith and credit of the U.S. government.
- Can readily be sold.
- Can lock in yields.

- If interest rates fall, potential for capital appreciation exists.

CONS

- If interest rates rise, the market price of your T-note will decline.
- If rates rise and you opt not to sell, you're locked in at the old, lower rate.

WHERE TO BUY

- Commercial banks, stockbrokers, by mail or directly from Federal Reserve Banks; the Bureau of Public Debt in Washington, DC. For Procedures on buying T-notes directly from the Bureau, call: 202-287-4900.

FEES

- Modest fee ($25–$50) charged by banks and brokers; no fee if purchased through a Federal Reserve Bank or from the Bureau of Public Debt.

RISK LEVEL

- Very high in safety; virtually no risk.

TAX IMPLICATIONS

- Interest exempt from state and local taxes.

KEEP IN MIND

- Interest rates are determined at auctions held periodically in Washington by the U.S. Treasury. These rates change depending upon the demand for money.
- Current yields are available by phoning the Bureau of Public Debt at 202-287-4100.
- T-bills can be used effectively to delay or avoid taxes in certain situations. If, for instance, you purchase a $10,000 T-bill in 1988 that matures in 1989, you won't be taxed (at the federal level) until the bill comes due. Use this technique if you have a lump sum of money coming due, say from the sale of a house or inheritance, and you want to delay paying taxes until the next year.
- The bonds will not be called (see page 26) for at least 25 years.

YOUR INVESTMENT PLANNER FOR U.S. TREASURY ISSUES

Type of bond: Purchased from:

Face amount: $ Number purchased: Fee: $ Total: $

Interest/coupon rate: Maturity date:

Potential call date: Where certificates held:

Call provision:

INTEREST INCOME

DATE	AMOUNT RECEIVED	TOTAL YEAR TO DATE

SALES & MATURITIES

DATE	PRINCIPAL AMOUNT	+	ACCRUED INTEREST	=	TOTAL AMOUNT

TAXES DUE

DATE	AMOUNT	DATE	AMOUNT

See page 54 for helpful formulas.

BANK SAVINGS ACCOUNTS

Yes, Virginia, there still is a savings account. But it's suggested only for small savers and small children.

If you have less than $250, using a bank savings account still makes sense; otherwise, use a money market mutual fund (see page 22) or money market bank deposit account (page 24). You'll have equal access to your money and earn much higher interest rates.

In 1986, 138 commercial banks and 21 savings & loans failed. Granted this is a small percentage of the total, but you certainly wouldn't have wanted your money in one of those 159 institutions. That's why insurance is so important. The federal government backs both FSLIC (Federal Savings & Loan Insurance Corp.), which insures deposits in S&Ls, and FDIC (Federal Deposit Insurance Corp.), which insures commercial banks. FDIC has a healthy $18.2 billion reserve fund, but FSLIC is not in such great shape: the General Accounting Office has declared it insolvent and Congress will have to bail it out with a $5 billion loan. So:

- Always bank at a federally insured institution.
- Keep your balance in each account under $100,000, leaving room for interest earnings.
- Diversify if you have over $100,000.
- Get an independent rating on your bank's financial strength from Veribanc, P.O. Box 2963, Woburn, MA 01888. Cost is $20 for a short report; $45 for a full-length study.

BEST FOR

- Small investors only.

MINIMUM INVESTMENT

- Varies from $1 to $100.

FOUR BASIC TYPES OF CHECKING ACCOUNTS

- DEMAND ACCOUNTS   You can make any number of deposits and write any number of checks and keep any balance. No interest.
- SuperNOW ACCOUNTS   You can write any number of checks but must maintain a certain minimum balance to earn interest. Interest rate changes, is higher than passbook and lower than money market rate.
- NOW ACCOUNTS   You can write any number of checks. Interest is the same as passbook rate. Smaller minimum balance than on SuperNOWs. Heavy fees if you fall below that minimum.
- MONEY MARKET ACCOUNTS   The number of checks you can write is restricted. Minimum balance is required. Highest interest rates.

KNOW HOW YOUR INTEREST IS COMPUTED

- DAY OF DEPOSIT TO DAY OF WITHDRAWAL   Best for you. Bank begins paying interest on your money as soon as it is deposited, even if there's a check that has been deposited but not yet cleared. Money earns interest right up to withdrawal.
- AVERAGE DAILY BALANCE   Almost as favorable as day of deposit to day of withdrawal. Bank adds up the balance in your account every day for a set number of days and then divides by that number of days.
- AVERAGE COLLECTED BALANCE   After daily balance in your account is added up, checks deposited and not yet collected are deducted and the result is divided by the number of days.
- LOW BALANCE   Interest is paid on the lowest balance during the time period, i.e., during the month.

PROS

- If federally insured, very safe.
- Can deposit any amount at any time.
- Passbook loan rates often low.

CONS

- The lowest interest rate of all savings vehicles.
- Fees can reduce yield to zero.

WHERE TO BUY

- Banks, savings & loans, credit unions.

FEES

- There may be fees for balances that fall below a stated minimum.
- Some banks do not pay interest if balance is below a stated dollar amount.
- Some banks limit number of free withdrawals per month and/or charge for extra withdrawals.

RISK LEVEL

- Low.

TAX IMPLICATIONS

- Interest earned is taxed as ordinary income.

YOUR INVESTMENT PLANNER FOR BANK SAVINGS ACCOUNTS

Location of passbook: Date opened:

Name of institution: Account #:

Address: Service charge?: Yes ___ No ___
                                                       Amount:
Telephone: Total yearly charge: $

Contact: Interest rate:
                                                       How compounded:

DEPOSITS	WITHDRAWALS	INTEREST EARNED	DATE	BALANCE

See page 54 for helpful formulas.

CERTIFICATES OF DEPOSIT (CDs)

This is short- to intermediate-term (1 month to 5 years) paper issued to the public by banks, savings & loans, and some credit unions. Interest may be paid monthly, quarterly, semiannually, or upon maturity. Interest rates may be fixed or variable. With a fixed-rate CD, the interest set when purchased remains the same until maturity. With a variable-rate CD, the interest is tied to an index, such as T-bill rates, and moves up and down along with the index. CDs are not negotiable; that is, they cannot be sold. Cashing them in prior to maturity entails a penalty.

BEST FOR

- Those who want ultimate safety and assured income.
- Holding cash or emergency reserves.
- Conservative IRAs.

FIXED CD
- Locking in interest rates if you feel they will decline.

VARIABLE CD
- Taking advantage of rising interest rates.

MINIMUM INVESTMENT

- Established by individual institutions; range tends to be from $500 to $10,000.

PROS

- Yields are competitive with money market accounts and T-bills.
- Because there's an early withdrawal penalty, you're less likely to spend money that's in a CD than money in a money market account.
- You can pick your own maturity date, staggering CDs to come due when you need money, say for college tuition or retirement.

CONS

- Your money is tied up until maturity.
- Rates may move up while your money is locked in at a lower level.
- Penalty for cashing in prior to maturity.

WHERE TO BUY

- Banks, savings & loans, credit unions, brokerage firms.

THE NEW BREED

In order to remain competitive with mutual funds and the stock market, banks have recently created CDs whose yields are tied to the performance of the S&P 500, the price of gold, prime rate, and even college costs. Some, called "bump-up" CDs, boost rates on a periodic basis. For details call your bank or:

CD	BANK	TELEPHONE
Chase Market Index CD	Chase Manhattan	800-245-1032
Gold Market CD	Wells Fargo	800-458-2583
S&P 500 CD	Fleet National	800-556-7988
Bump-up CD	Crossland Savings	718-780-0400
Prime Rate CD	Landmark Banks	314-889-1600
College Costs CD	College Savings Bank	800-342-6670
Bear Market CD	Chase Lincoln	716-258-5000

FEES

- None.

RISK LEVEL

- Low; high in safety.
- Insured for up to $100,000 at institutions that are FDIC or FSLIC insured (make sure your money is in one).

TAX IMPLICATIONS

- Interest is taxed as ordinary income when CD matures.

KEEP IN MIND

- Shop around before purchasing; rates vary widely from one institution to another.
- Ask about rollover procedures and how often interest is computed; daily is best (see box on page 18).
- To find out which banks pay the best rates, consult the current issue of *Money* magazine.
- To determine a bank's safety level, contact: Veribanc, P.O. Box 2963, Woburn, MA 01888. They will send you a short financial report for $20; a full-length report for $45.

YOUR INVESTMENT PLANNER FOR CERTIFICATES OF DEPOSIT (CDs)

Name of bank:

Address:

Telephone:

Contact:

Account number:

Rollover provisions:

Penalty for early withdrawal:

AMOUNT	DATE PURCHASED	INTEREST RATE AND HOW COMPOUNDED	TERM/DATE DUE	BALANCE AT MATURITY

See page 54 for helpful formulas.

MONEY MARKET MUTUAL FUNDS

A mutual fund is an investment company that pools money from thousands of individuals to buy shares in various investment vehicles and securities. This money is professionally invested by a fund manager who continually studies the market, interest rate fluctuations, and the overall economic climate. He or she buys and sells investments that meet the mutual fund's stated objectives. In the case of a money market mutual fund, the objective is interest income and safety, or maximum return with minimum risk. The term *money market* was chosen because this type of fund invests in a variety of short-term, relatively safe money market instruments, including Treasury bills, commercial paper, bankers acceptances, and jumbo CDs. Interest rates vary daily depending on the mixture in the fund's portfolio and overall market conditions. Dividends are paid monthly to shareholders.

BEST FOR

- Parking extra cash you may want to use in the near future.
- Investors who have active brokerage accounts and sell securities on a regular basis.

MINIMUM INVESTMENT

- Established by each fund; typically $1,000, with shares priced at $1 each.

PROS

- Can add or withdraw money at any time without a penalty or a fee.
- Competitive interest rates.
- Professional management.
- Check-writing privileges often available.
- Do not have to maintain a minimum balance.

KEEP IN MIND

Two funds have no minimum deposit requirements: First Trust Money Market Mutual Fund (800-621-4770) and Cash & Plus Trust (800-345-1151). For a free, complete list of mutual funds, write:

Investment Company Institute
1600 M Street, NW
Washington, DC 20036

For everything you need to know about no-load funds, write for:

"The Handbook for No-Load Fund Investors,"
1987 edition
P.O. Box 283
Hastings-on-Hudson, NY 10706
$36

FINDING A FUND

You will find a listing of money market mutual funds in the financial pages of the newspaper. The current yield, one-week yield, and assets are usually given. Call your broker for details on the fund the firm uses or contact one of these high-yielding funds:

FIVE TOP TAXABLE MONEY MARKET FUNDS
E. F. Hutton Cash Fund
Fidelity Cash Reserves
Kemper Money Market
Kemper Liquid Trust
Merrill Lynch Ready Assets

FIVE TOP TAX-FREE MONEY MARKET FUNDS
Calvert Tax-Free Reserves
Franklin Tax-Exempt
Shearson Lehman Daily Tax-Free
T. Rowe Price Tax-Exempt
Vanguard Muni Bond Money Market

CONS

- Not federally insured as are bank money market deposit accounts.
- Yield fluctuates, a disadvantage when rates decline.
- Many funds restrict withdrawals to a certain dollar amount.

WHERE TO BUY

- Directly from the fund, stockbrokers, or brokerage service subsidiaries of some banks and S&Ls.

FEES

- None.

RISK LEVEL

- Although not federally insured, money funds are high in safety.
- For ultimate safety, buy shares in one of the funds that invest only in U.S. government securities, or those whose holdings mature in less than 40 days. This means your money will earn current rates, an advantage if rates rise.
- A few funds are insured.

TAX IMPLICATIONS

- Interest is taxed as ordinary income in the year it is earned unless you purchase shares in a tax-exempt fund.

YOUR INVESTMENT PLANNER FOR MONEY MARKET MUTUAL FUNDS

Name of fund: Telephone:

Account number:

PURCHASE PRICE	# OF SHARES	TOTAL COST	DIVIDEND REINVESTED	TOTAL SHARES	YIELD

To keep track of the daily yield, call the Fund's 800 number. For the weekly yield, check the business section of your newspaper for the 7-day average yield. The average monthly yield will appear on the statement you receive.

INTEREST RATE/YIELD

Jan _____   Feb _____   Mar _____   Apr _____   May _____   Je _____

Jly _____   Aug _____   Sep _____   Oct _____   Nov _____   Dec _____

MONEY MARKET BANK DEPOSIT ACCOUNTS

In the early 1980s, deregulation in the banking industry allowed banks to establish a new type of account that competed directly with the by-then extremely popular money market mutual funds. Initially, in an effort to lure away customers from the funds, these bank accounts paid higher rates of interest. Since then, however, their rates have fallen, so that today most are lower than those offered by the funds.

Money market bank deposit accounts and money market mutual funds remain quite similar, with rates on both moving up and down with short-term yields. However, there are some distinct differences besides interest rates, which you should take into consideration when deciding where to park your hard-earned dollars.

- In most cases, when the balance in a money market bank account drops below the set minimum (typically $2,500), the interest rate also drops, often to the paltry 5½% passbook rate. This is not true of money market mutual funds, since very few require a minimum balance.
- Money market bank accounts are federally insured. Funds are not.
- Banks are stickier about check-writing. Typically, if you write more than three checks in one month your interest rate will suffer. Money market mutual funds tend to have unlimited check-writing and seldom levy fees or penalties.
- It's usually easier to do business with your bank, especially if it's in your neighborhood or near where you work.

Select a money market bank account that:

- Has no service or transaction costs.
- Requires no minimum transaction amounts.
- Computes interest using the day of deposit to day of withdrawal method.

BEST FOR

- Savers who want immediate access to their money.
- Those who prefer doing business with their bank rather than a mutual fund.

MINIMUM INVESTMENT

- $1,500, $2,000, or $2,500, depending upon bank.

PROS

- Each depositor is federally insured for up to $100,000 if institution carries FCIC or FSLIC insurance (see page 18 on bank safety).
- Immediate access to funds.
- No withdrawal penalty.
- Limitation on number of checks you can write encourages saving.

CONS

- Must maintain minimum balance to receive highest interest rate.
- Institutions limit you to three checks per month, which means you still need to maintain a checking account.
- Automatic transfers and telephone withdrawals to another account or to third parties generally limited to three per month.
- Higher rates usually available in money market mutual funds, CDs, and many bonds.

WHERE TO BUY

- Banks, S&Ls, credit unions.

FEES

- Ranges from zero to a few dollars per month.

RISK LEVEL

- Very low.

TAX IMPLICATIONS

- Interest is subject to federal, state, and local taxes in the year it is earned.

MONEY MARKET MUTUAL FUND VS. MONEY MARKET BANK ACCOUNT

Use the points listed here to do your own comparison study and determine the best place to open a money market account. After you've made your choice, reevaluate it at least once a year or when you receive a notice that the terms of the account are changing.

- Minimum to open
- Minimum subsequent deposits
- Minimum balance to earn top rate
- Method used to compute balance
- Method used to compute interest
- When interest is computed
- Average interest rate paid last year
- Average interest rate paid last 6 months
- Current yield
- Minimum check size
- Minimum/maximum withdrawal
- Maximum number of withdrawals by check, by transfer, and in person
- Service charges
- Fees for transactions

YOUR INVESTMENT PLANNER FOR MONEY MARKET BANK DEPOSIT ACCOUNTS

Name of institution:

Address:

Telephone:

Contact:

Account #:

Minimum opening balance: $

Minimum subsequent balance: $

Service charge?: Yes ___ No ___
    Amount:

Interest rate:
    How compounded:

DEPOSITS	WITHDRAWALS	INTEREST EARNED	DATE	BALANCE

See page 54 for helpful formulas.

CORPORATE BONDS

When corporations want to raise capital, one of the ways they do so is by selling bonds to investors with the promise to pay back the face value of the bond at the date of maturity plus interest. The corporation sets the interest rate (called the coupon rate), which is fixed in keeping with the cost of money at the time of issue. Bonds can be issued for almost any number of years, although the maximum is generally 30. Those with maturity dates under 10 years are called notes.

When reading the bond quotes in the paper, you'll see that they are not quoted at $1,000 (face value) but rather on the basis of a par of 100, so always add another zero to the figure to get the cash price you must pay.

Although bonds are still recommended primarily for income, the recent volatility of the bond market has become an important consideration. If interest rates rise and you need to sell your bonds prior to maturity, you'll face a loss because the value of your bonds will have dropped. This volatility makes it all the more important to keep track of your bonds on your worksheets.

Many American corporations issue bonds on a continual basis. They tend to pay higher yields than U.S. Treasuries because they are not backed by the government and thus are considerably higher in risk. You can easily determine the quality of a bond by checking its rating in Moody's or Standard & Poor's. Stick to AA or AAA ratings to reduce the chance of default. And by purchasing intermediate maturities you'll avoid interest rate risk—the risk that rates will go up while you're locked in to issues with lower yields.

BEST FOR

- Investors seeking regular income.
- Meeting long-term goals.

MINIMUM INVESTMENT

- $1,000 face amount; same for most bond mutual funds.

PROS

- Offer steady stream of fixed income.
- Price appreciation if interest rates fall.
- Can lock in high yields long term.
- Can sell at any time in secondary market.
- Wide range of maturities to select from.
- Guaranteed return of principal if held to maturity.

CONS

- If interest rates rise, value of bond will decline.
- If corporation runs into financial trouble, bond could drop in price.
- Issuer could default on interest payments or principal or both.
- Can be called early.
- No inflation protection.
- Expensive to sell small lots.

WHERE TO BUY

- Stockbrokers or bond mutual funds.

FEES

- Tend to be high; brokers charge minimums of $25 to $50 per bond but give better rates for larger orders.

RISK LEVEL

- Varies depending on Standard & Poor's or Moody's rating; generally only moderately risky, except for junk bonds, which are very risky.

TAX IMPLICATIONS

- Interest earned is taxed at federal, state, and local levels.

BOND BASICS

- **CALL PROVISION**   Allows the issuer to redeem the bond prior to scheduled maturity date. Bonds have a *call price*, which is usually higher than the face value in order to compensate the bond owner for the loss of future interest income. You can tell if a bond is callable by the way it is listed: 2000–2017 means the bond matures in the year 2017 but can be called in 2000 or any time thereafter.
- **COUPON**   The interest rate paid on a bond until the bond reaches maturity. For instance, a bond with an 8% coupon pays $8 per $100 of the face value per year. Coupons are clipped from the bond and presented to the issuer for collection of the interest, which is due semiannually.
- **DISCOUNT BOND**   A bond that sells below its face value.
- **FACE VALUE**   This is the amount the owner of a bond receives when the bond is redeemed at maturity. Also known as par value. It appears on the face of the bond.
- **PREMIUM BOND**   A bond that sells above its face value.

YOUR INVESTMENT PLANNER FOR CORPORATE BONDS

Name of issuer:

Type of bond:

Rating:

Interest/coupon rate:

Maturity date: Purchased through:

Potential call date: Where certificates held:

Call provision:

Face amount: $ Number purchased: Fee: $ Total: $

INTEREST INCOME

DATE	AMOUNT RECEIVED	TOTAL YEAR TO DATE

SALES & MATURITIES

DATE	PRINCIPAL AMOUNT	+	ACCRUED INTEREST	=	TOTAL AMOUNT

INTEREST RECEIVED

DATE	AMOUNT	DATE	AMOUNT

MUNICIPAL BONDS

It's no fun to pay taxes, and since the passage of the Tax Reform Act of 1986 there are far fewer ways to shelter income from the IRS. But one perfectly legitimate solution that remains is municipal bonds. Interest on these bonds, issued by state and local governments, is exempt from federal income tax and from state and local taxes in the state where the bonds are issued. Governments issue these bonds to raise money to build roads, bridges, and schools and to finance local projects. Although they pay lower rates than regular bonds, their yields may actually be higher when you compare them to the after-tax yields of taxable bonds (see page 71).

Municipals come in a large range of maturity dates, from 1 to about 30 years. The longest ones pay the highest rates but are subject to the greatest interest rate risk.

Tax reform created two new groups of munis—fully taxable issues and partially taxables. Private purpose bonds (also known as industrial development bonds) are municipal bonds in which more than 10% of the proceeds go to a private development. If issued after August 7, 1986, their income is subject to the alternative minimum tax (AMT). If your income is sufficiently high, you might be socked with the new tax, so check with your accountant.

To add to the confusion, there are also fully taxable municipals, such as bonds for pollution control facilities, convention centers, industrial parks, and shopping malls. Although these are now subject to federal tax, they remain exempt from state tax.

Don't automatically reject a taxable muni—they have three distinct advantages: (1) They tend to yield as much as 1½% more than Treasuries of comparable maturities and 2 to 3% more than tax-exempt municipals. (2) They have shorter maturities, usually 10 years. (3) They are not callable.

KEEP IN MIND

- The place for taxable munis, which combine safety and income, is in your IRA or Keogh.
- Use zero coupon municipals with relatively short maturities (10 years) to finance your child's education.
- Buy double- or triple-exempt bonds; these are exempt from state and local taxes in the state issued, which is particularly important to those living in states with high personal income tax rates.
- To be on the safe side, buy municipals that are AAA-rated or insured. Although very few munis have gone into default, it's best to take the added precaution.

Regardless of which type of muni you buy, they are subject to interest rate risk. The best way to protect yourself is to: (1) buy shorter maturities (7 to 10 years), (2) stagger maturity dates, or (3) buy shares in a municipal bond fund where the portfolio is continually adjusted in anticipation of interest rate changes. A final choice is investment trusts (see page 30).

BEST FOR

- Those in higher tax brackets seeking tax-free income.

MINIMUM INVESTMENT

- $5,000.

PROS

- One of the few tax shelters left.
- High after-tax yields.
- If interest rates fall, opportunity for capital appreciation.
- Many choices of maturity date.
- Some are insured.

CONS

- Always a chance of default.
- If interest rates rise, value of bonds falls.
- Spread between taxable and tax-exempt returns has narrowed since tax reform.
- Lowering of tax brackets makes them less appealing than before the new tax law.

WHERE TO BUY

- Stockbrokers, bond dealers.

FEES

- Generally 2 to 3% of bond's price.
- No fee for new bonds if purchased from the underwriter.

RISK LEVEL

- Fairly low.
- Insured bonds are available, paying about ½ less than noninsured issues.

TAX IMPLICATIONS

- As explained above.

YOUR INVESTMENT PLANNER FOR MUNICIPAL BONDS

Name of issuer:

Type of bond:

Rating:

Interest/coupon rate:

Maturity date: Purchased through:

Potential call date: Where certificates held:

Call provision:

Tax exempt?: Yes _____
              No _____
   If yes, at what level:

Face amount: $ Number purchased: Fee: $ Total: $

INTEREST INCOME

DATE	AMOUNT RECEIVED	TOTAL YEAR TO DATE

SALES & MATURITIES

DATE	PRINCIPAL AMOUNT	+	ACCRUED INTEREST	=	TOTAL AMOUNT

INTEREST RECEIVED

DATE	AMOUNT	DATE	AMOUNT

UNIT INVESTMENT TRUSTS

A close cousin of the more popular mutual fund is the unit investment trust in which individuals can purchase shares (units) for as little as $1,000. The money is invested in a fixed portfolio of income-producing securities. Whereas in a mutual fund (see page 38) the portfolio continually changes as the manager buys and sells securities, in a unit investment trust the portfolio typically remains fixed except for an occasional review. Since it is unmanaged, this type of investment charges a lower administrative fee, in some cases none at all.

Each unit trust concentrates on a particular type of fixed-income security, such as municipal bonds, corporate bonds, government bonds, CDs, or government-backed mortgages. There are also a handful of equity or stock-based trusts, some consisting of public utility stocks with strong dividends. Portfolios are closed-end, which means there are only a limited number of units for sale. (A mutual fund, on the other hand, is open-end and continually offering new shares to the public.)

When you buy a unit trust, the prospectus details its holdings. What you see is what you get—although the trust reserves the right to sell a security that is in deep trouble, in general the portfolio stands as is until the securities mature or are called. Therefore it is a self-liquidating investment. The average trust runs 25 years, although some run only 6 months, others 30 years. Upon maturity, the securities are sold or redeemed and you get back all your capital.

The yield, like the portfolio, is set for the length of the trust. Interest income and dividends are passed on to unit holders on a regular basis and, as the bonds mature, the proceeds are also distributed. Don't be surprised if your checks are not the same every month. As bonds mature or are called, this activity is reflected in the checks you receive. This monthly fluctuation does not reduce the amount you receive upon maturity.

Although the diversification offered by a unit trust obviously reduces your risk, many sponsors boost the safety factor by obtaining insurance to guarantee both principal and repayment of principal of bonds in a trust. It reduces the yield by about ½%.

A number of unit trusts allow investors to automatically reinvest both interest and principal distributions in a mutual fund managed by the trust sponsors. This not only eliminates the problem of where to reinvest interest income, it also provides a means of forced savings. Some unit trusts allow switching between trusts run by the same sponsor. Others have check-writing privileges.

BEST FOR

- Small investors seeking a steady flow of fixed income and preservation of capital.

MINIMUM INVESTMENT

- $1,000.

PROS

- Can lock in high yield for long term; receive regular income checks.
- Lower minimum than if you bought bonds on your own; for $1,000 you own a package of 10 to 35 issues.
- May be able to reinvest dividends automatically.
- Smaller management fee than with a mutual fund.
- Get back principal upon maturity.

CONS

- Portfolio not actively managed.
- Sales charges higher than with a no-load fund.
- Units can be sold back to sponsor, but no active secondary market in traditional sense.

WHERE TO BUY

- Stockbrokers and broker/dealers.

FEES

- Sales charges range from 3 to 5½% of principal paid.
- Annual administrative fees of ¼%, expressed as part of yield quoted to prospective buyers.

RISK LEVEL

- Medium to low (check ratings of bonds as well as call provisions in the prospectus prior to purchase).
- Can buy an insured tax-exempt trust with a slightly lower yield—½%—than uninsured trusts.

TAX IMPLICATIONS

- Municipal bond unit trusts usually exempt from federal taxes and single-state trusts from state and local taxes.
- In other trusts, interest income, dividends, and distribution of principal are taxed; however, there are many varieties of trusts, so check with your accountant before purchasing.

YOUR INVESTMENT PLANNER FOR UNIT INVESTMENT TRUSTS

Name: Interest rate:

Series number: Maturity date:

Purchased from: Purchase price:
                                         Sales charge:

Telephone: Date purchased:

Name of sales rep./broker: Tax exempt?: Yes _____
                                                       No _____
                                         If yes, at what level:

CHECKS RECEIVED

PRINCIPAL	INTEREST
Date: _____	_____
Date: _____	_____
Date: _____	_____
Date: _____	_____
Total for year: _____	_____
Principal reinvested: _____	_____
Where: _____	_____
Yield: _____	_____

ZERO COUPON BONDS

An investment where you only need to spend $200 to buy a bond worth $1,000? It's possible with a fixed-income security called a zero coupon bond. It's called a zero because, unlike a regular bond, it does not come with interest rate coupons—they've been stripped off. That means you don't receive regular interest payments but instead buy the zero at a deep discount (as much as 50 to 70% of face value) and collect the full face value upon maturity. Up until that time there's absolutely zero income. The interest on a zero, therefore, is the difference between the cash purchase price and the full face value paid out at maturity. In that respect zeros are like savings bonds (see page 14) and T-bills (page 16), although in both those investments you can defer taxes until redeemed.

There are a myriad of zeros on the market. They're offered by corporations, municipalities, and even the U.S. Treasury. Not only are they an inexpensive way to invest but they have another key advantage: you know exactly how much you'll receive upon maturity.

Zeros also have their downside: You must pay taxes on the interest every year just as though you had received it. And unless you plan to hold them until maturity, don't buy them. They are extremely volatile in price, and just when you might want to sell they may have dropped in price.

BEST FOR

- Meeting a long-range goal such as college tuition, retirement, buying a house, etc.
- IRA, Keogh, or other tax-sheltered accounts.

MINIMUM INVESTMENT

- Varies from issue to issue; generally 50 to 70% of face value.

PROS

- You know your precise return.
- You don't need to worry about where to reinvest the interest income since you receive it upon maturity; this is a great advantage during periods when interest rates are declining.
- Upfront investment is small.

CONS

- You must pay taxes on the interest as it accrues annually, just as though you had received it. Exception: municipal zeros.
- You're locked into an interest rate, which is a disadvantage if rates rise.

- With all but the safest of bonds, there's always a chance of default.
- Bonds may be called early, although it's less likely than with regular bonds because the issuer is not paying out interest.
- Zeros are more volatile in price than most bonds; therefore they're best held to maturity.

WHERE TO BUY

- Stockbrokers.

FEES

- Vary; inquire first; typically 2 to 6% of purchase price.

RISK LEVEL

- Varies with issuing body; corporate zeros are riskier than U.S. Treasury zeros issued by brokerage houses.
- Check bond ratings in Moody's or Standard & Poor's.

TAX IMPLICATIONS

- Taxes must be paid on interest earned by corporate zeros even though it's not received until maturity.
- This distinct disadvantage means corporate zeros are best in IRAs or Keoghs where interest income is not reported until withdrawn.
- Municipal zeros are exempt from federal taxes plus state and local taxes if issued in purchaser's state; they should *not* be placed in your IRA or Keogh.
- Corporate zeros are also suitable for children's accounts if children are age 14 and in a lower tax bracket than you.
- Treasury zeros are exempt from state and local taxes.

MEETING FINANCIAL GOALS WITH ZEROS

Treasury zeros, the safest of all zeros, are excellent for long-range planning. Buy them with maturities staggered to come due each year you face a large expense. For example, a $1,000 face value Treasury zero with a 9% coupon maturing in 1991 would cost $638.41. In 1991 you would receive the full $1,000. The more distant the maturity date, the less you pay.

YOUR INVESTMENT PLANNER FOR ZERO COUPON BONDS

Name of issuer:

Type of bond:

Rating:

Interest/coupon rate:

Maturity date: Purchased through:

Potential call date: Where certificates held:

Call provision:

Face amount: $ Number purchased: Fee: $ Total: $

INTEREST INCOME

DATE	AMOUNT RECEIVED	TOTAL YEAR TO DATE

SALES & MATURITIES

DATE	PRINCIPAL AMOUNT	+	ACCRUED INTEREST	=	TOTAL AMOUNT

TAXES DUE

DATE	AMOUNT	DATE	AMOUNT

See page 54 for helpful formulas.

JUNK BONDS

If you're looking for very high income, tantalizing yields, a way to double your money, and you don't mind taking on equally high risk, look into the so-called junk bonds, Wall Street's name for bonds of financially troubled companies.

Junk bonds, which are ranked below investment grade (BB or lower by Standard & Poor's and Ba or lower by Moody's), are definitely not for the faint-hearted. These low ratings reflect the concern of the two independent bond-rating services that the issuers may not have the ability to cover interest payments, principal when due at maturity, or both. Because of their questionable strength, junk bonds often sell at a huge discount from face value.

The junk bond universe consists of older corporations that previously had sound reputations; companies financing takeovers of other companies; corporations financing buybacks or self-tenders of their own stock; or managements financing leveraged buyouts. Low ratings are also assigned to many new companies that have not yet had to post a record of earnings.

Yet not all junk bonds are in fact really junk. If the company issuing the bonds is basically sound, the lower debt rating may be temporary, in which case it could be an excellent buying opportunity for investors not adverse to risk. If later on the company's earnings improve, its debt is reduced, and the ratings subsequently go up, investors could see substantial price appreciation. Look for a company with improving cash flow. Try also to discover whether management has plans to sell certain assets, cut expenses, or improve efficiency, all of which will help boost its credit rating.

Consider investing in a high-yield mutual fund where professional management combined with a widely diversified portfolio greatly reduce risk.

BEST FOR

- Investors with excess cash seeking a high yield who are comfortable with high risk.

MINIMUM INVESTMENT

- Several hundred dollars per bond for those selling at a discount.
- $1,000 in a mutual fund.

PROS

- Exceptionally high yields.
- Potential for impressive price appreciation.
- Available at significant discounts.

CONS

- Highly speculative.
- Interest payments and coverage of principal at risk unless company's financial strength improves.
- If company enters bankruptcy, you could lose your entire investment.

WHERE TO BUY

- Stockbrokers, mutual funds.

FEES

- Usual brokerage commission.
- Fund fees vary; check prospectus first.

RISK LEVEL

- Very high.

TAX IMPLICATIONS

- Interest and dividends subject to state, local, and federal taxes.

BOND RATINGS: WHAT THEY STAND FOR		
S&P RATING	DEFINITION	MOODY'S RATING
AAA	Highest rating with lowest degree of risk: U.S. Treasury and government agency bonds, Exxon, IBM.	Aaa
AA	High quality but less protection: AT&T, Mobil.	Aa
A	Upper medium quality: Westinghouse, ITT.	A
BBB	Medium grade; interest and principal secure now but long-term not guaranteed: Occidental Petroleum, Burroughs.	Baa
BB	Speculative; future cannot be assured: Long Island Lighting.	Ba
B	Below investment grade; no assurance of future interest payments: Bethlehem Steel, Navistar Int'l.	B
CCC CC C	Highly speculative or in default: Western Union, Texas Air.	Caa CC C

YOUR INVESTMENT PLANNER FOR JUNK BONDS

Use this worksheet if you purchase junk bonds through a mutual fund. If you purchase a junk bond outside of a mutual fund, use the worksheet for corporate bonds on page 27.

Name of issuer or fund: Mutual fund name (if any):

Address: Telephone:

Account number: Switching fee:

Distribution date: Redemption fee:

PURCHASES

DATE PURCHASED	# OF SHARES	PRICE/ SHARE	FEE	DIVIDEND REINVEST.	TOTAL $ INC. FEES	VALUE ON 12/31

SALES

DATE SOLD	# OF SHARES	TOTAL AMOUNT	PROFIT OR LOSS	TAX SITUATION

To keep track of the daily yield, call the Fund's 800 number. For the weekly yield, check the business section of your newspaper for the 7-day average yield. The average monthly yield will appear on the statement you receive.

YIELD			TOTAL RETURN		
Jan _____	May _____	Sep _____	Jan _____	May _____	Sep _____
Feb _____	Je _____	Oct _____	Feb _____	Je _____	Oct _____
Mar _____	Jly _____	Nov _____	Mar _____	Jly _____	Nov _____
Apr _____	Aug _____	Dec _____	Apr _____	Aug _____	Dec _____

See page 54 for helpful formulas.

STOCKS

Louis Rukeyser, host of the popular financial TV show "Wall Street Week," is fond of saying, "In Wall Street the only thing that's hard to explain is next week."

That's why you must continually keep track of your stocks: know what you bought, when you bought it, and at what price. By faithful monitoring of your portfolio, whether it's 10 shares or 10,000, you'll be able to determine whether to buy, sell, or simply hold.

If you're going to play the stock market, remember the following elementary concepts and skip right over those complicated theories, hot tips, and wild rumors heard at the gym or tennis club.

- A common stock is a security that represents fractional ownership in a corporation.
- There are three things this stock can do: it can go up in price; it can do down; or it can stay the same.
- There are two ways to make money with a stock: through price appreciation and through dividends. A company pays cash dividends when directors vote to give shareholders a part of the profits. Whatever isn't paid out in dividends is plowed back into the company. Shares appreciate when earnings increase, when profits are up, and when the perception of future growth is positive.

KEYS TO PICKING THE BEST STOCKS

- **BOOK VALUE**   Net asset value of a company, or what the company would be worth if all its assets were sold, debts paid, and the net proceeds distributed to the shareholders. Stocks selling below book value may be undervalued and eventually rise in price and/or be taken over. (See Formulas, page 54.)
- **PRICE/EARNINGS RATIO**   Price of a stock divided by earnings per share. Listed in the newspaper with the stock quotes. The P/E ratio tells you how much you are paying for earning power. Low P/Es may indicate a bargain; very high P/Es may signal over-zealous buying. The average P/E for the S&P 500 is 22.
- **RETURN ON EQUITY**   A measure of a company's profitability, determined by dividing earnings by book value. It tells you how well management is doing with retained profits (those not paid out in dividends). For example, 5% is low, 20% impressive.
- **CASH FLOW PER SHARE**   Net income plus depreciation and other noncash charges. If a stock sells at 5 times cash flow it indicates a strong financial position.

- There are two ways to lose money with a stock: by holding it too long and by selling it too soon.

HOW TRACKING PREVENTS LOSSES

People tend to hold onto a stock long after it's peaked and fallen in price either because they're greedy or because they're not closely charting its progress. If your stock has a substantial price rise, take a closer look. Are the fundamental reasons why you purchased it still valid? If not, sell and take the profit. Set percentage limits on declines and learn to cut your losses.

BEST FOR

- Those who have already established a nest egg.

MINIMUM INVESTMENT

- Price of one share of stock plus commission.
- It's cheaper to buy in round lots of 100 shares.

PROS

- No limit on stock or dividend increases.
- Provides some protection against inflation.
- Instant liquidity.

CONS

- Can lose some or all of your investment.
- Not insured or guaranteed.
- Time-consuming; you need to follow the market.

WHERE TO BUY

- Stockbrokers, company dividend reinvestment plans, mutual funds, bank brokerage subsidiaries, investment clubs.

FEES

- Commissions set by individual brokerage firms and depend on the size of your order.

RISK LEVEL

- Relatively high compared with Treasury issues, CDs, and fixed-income investments.

TAX IMPLICATIONS

- All dividend income and capital gains (or loss) are taxed in the year received.
- Losses can be used to offset capital gains and up to $3,000 of ordinary income and salary.

YOUR INVESTMENT PLANNER FOR STOCKS

Name of corporation: ☐ Common ☐ Preferred

Purchased
   through broker:
   direct from company:
   by reinvestment of dividends:
   with investment club:

Where certificates held:

Stock splits?: Yes _____ No _____
   If yes, effective date:
      number shares now owned:
      new price per share:

PURCHASES

DATE PURCHASED	# OF SHARES	PRICE/SHARE	TOTAL $	COMMISSION	VALUE ON 12/31

SALES

DATE SOLD	# SHARES SOLD	PRICE/SHARE	$ PROFIT/LOSS

DIVIDEND INCOME

DATE	AMOUNT	DATE	AMOUNT

See page 54 for helpful formulas.

MUTUAL FUNDS

You don't have to be a Rockefeller, Donald Trump, or Rupert Murdoch to hire a professional to manage your portfolio. You can have a money manager for as little as $250 or certainly $1,000. How? By buying shares in a mutual fund. And you'll have lots of company: they have total assets in excess of $800 billion.

A mutual fund is an open-end investment company because it continually offers new shares for sale upon demand. These funds pool thousands of investors' dollars to buy a diversified portfolio that is carefully invested by a professional team.

Some funds buy stocks, while others focus on bonds; many buy a mixture. Some funds concentrate on a particular industry such as real estate or utilities, others on convertible bonds or government securities. Many are very conservative while some are intentionally speculative in hopes of making a big killing.

The advantages to this pooled approach are many, but essentially a fund allows you to buy fractional shares of many more stocks or bonds than you could afford on your own, and it dramatically reduces your risk level. If several shares in a fund drop sharply in price, the total impact on the fund (which may have 100 or 150 issues in its portfolio) is still minimal.

As a fund shareholder you can make money in one of four ways: from dividend income, interest income, profits from the sale of the fund's securities (also known as capital gains), and, if the value of the securities held by the fund rises, an increase in the value of your mutual fund shares.

Funds pay shareholders quarterly dividends and distribute any profits made from the sale of securities on an annual basis. This latter is known as a capital gains distribution.

Note: Yield is the amount of dividend and interest income paid to shareholders per share. *Total return* measures the per share change in the fund's total value during a given time period, often 1 month, 6 months, or one year. It includes interest income, dividends, and capital gains or losses.

BEST FOR

- Those who want professional guidance.
- Small investors who want a diversified portfolio.
- Those unable to do their own research.

MINIMUM INVESTMENT

- $250 to $1,000.

PROS

- Diversification of portfolio holdings.

- Full-time professional management.
- Automatic reinvestment of dividends.
- Opportunity to switch within a family of funds.
- Can make subsequent purchases for as little as $25.
- Can sell shares immediately.
- Designed to meet various goals and risk levels.

CONS

- Return is not guaranteed.
- Value of your shares could decline.
- Dividend payments could be reduced.
- Portfolio manager may misjudge the market.
- Sales charges can eat into profits.

WHERE TO BUY

- *No-load funds:* directly from the fund
- *Load funds:* from stockbrokers

FEES

- *No-load funds:* None; however, there may be a back-end load ranging from 1 to 6% for withdrawing money.
- *Load funds:* Varies with broker, but there's always a fee for purchases; it may be as much as 8.5% of your initial investment.
- A hidden fee, known as a 12(b)1, can be levied to cover advertising and sales cost; it must be so listed in the prospectus.
- Switch fees may be $5 or $10.
- A management fee is paid by the fund to those managing the fund's portfolio. Average is ½% a year of the fund's total assets. This fee and other expenses total between 1 and 1½%. They are paid from the fund's assets and are reflected in the price of the fund's shares.
- Ask if the fund has a breakpoint: if you invest a large enough amount you will receive lower fees.
- If you are uncertain about the fees involved, call the fund directly.

(*Note:* There is no data to support the contention by salespeople that load funds are superior to no-loads. Therefore, if you have time to do your own research, select a no-load and save on the various fees.)

RISK LEVEL

- From safe to risky, depending on fund.

TAX IMPLICATIONS

- Depends on type of fund and state where you live.

YOUR INVESTMENT PLANNER FOR MUTUAL FUNDS

Name of fund: Mutual fund name (if any):

Address: Telephone:

                                                 Switching fee:

Account number: Redemption fee:

Name of account holder: Distribution date:

PURCHASES

DATE PURCHASED	# OF SHARES	PRICE/ SHARE	FEE	DIVIDEND REINVEST.	TOTAL $ INCL. FEES	VALUE ON 12/31

SALES

DATE SOLD	# OF SHARES	TOTAL AMOUNT	PROFIT OR LOSS	TAX SITUATION

To keep track of the daily yield, call the Fund's 800 number. For the weekly yield, check the business section of your newspaper for the 7-day average yield. The average monthly yield will appear on the statement you receive.

YIELD				TOTAL RETURN		
Jan _____	May _____	Sep _____		Jan _____	May _____	Sep _____
Feb _____	Je _____	Oct _____		Feb _____	Je _____	Oct _____
Mar _____	Jly _____	Nov _____		Mar _____	Jly _____	Nov _____
Apr _____	Aug _____	Dec _____		Apr _____	Aug _____	Dec _____

See page 54 for helpful formulas.

GINNIE MAES (GNMAs)

Ginnie Mae is a nickname for Government National Mortgage Association, a U.S. government–owned corporation designed to promote housing by raising continual capital for mortgages. Ginnie Maes are mortgaged-backed securities that represent part ownership of pools of mortgage loans.

Ginnie Mae sells certificates (or pieces of these pools) to investors in denominations of $25,000 each. As homeowners pay back their mortgages to their banks, Ginnie Mae passes through this money (both interest and principal) to owners of certificates in the form of monthly checks. Since mortgages mature at various times and since they are paid off at different rates, the Ginnie Mae investor receives an uneven flow of cash. Monthly payments are based on the amount of principal left each month in the pool. Although Ginnie Maes are basically 30-year securities, they trade with an assumed average life of 12 years.

If you like the advantages of a Ginnie Mae but do not wish to invest $25,000, you can buy shares in a *Ginnie Mae Mutual Fund,* where the minimum required is typically only $1,000. These funds are professionally managed, and your principal and interest can be reinvested automatically in new fund shares.

Ginnie Mae funds, nevertheless, have certain risks you should understand. If mortgages are paid off early, the fund manager is forced to reinvest the fund's portfolio in newer certificates, which may pay lower rates. Your yield will obviously drop in this case. The value of your shares may also decline: if your fund paid above par, say 110, for certificates with a high yield, and these are being paid off early at par (100), your shares will fall in value.

Some funds also invest in more speculative securities that do not carry the full government guarantee. Or they may use speculative techniques to boost their yield—such as hedging, selling options against the portfolio, or buying interest rate futures contracts. These ploys boost yields but they likewise boost the risk level. The fund's prospectus will list such techniques as well as what is in the portfolio.

If you buy certificates in the secondary market, note that some may have lower coupon rates than new certificates. These have already been partially paid down. When interest rates fall, older certificates sell above par because their higher yields make them more attractive. However, the risk of early prepayments and subsequent reduced yields is always present, and predicting prepayment speed is difficult even for experts.

BEST FOR

- Those who want a steady stream of income with relative safety.

MINIMUM INVESTMENT

- $25,000 per certificate with $5,000 increments.
- $1,000 in a Ginnie Mae mutual fund.

PROS

- Yields are typically about 1% higher than U.S. Treasury bills of the same maturity.
- Provide monthly income.
- Can be sold at any time in secondary market.

CONS

- Monthly payments are *not* uniform and may decrease as homeowners pay off their mortgages.
- Over the long run, a Ginnie Mae certificate is self-liquidating; it is not a permanent investment, so unless you invest your checks elsewhere, say in a money market fund, there will be no money at the end of the payments.
- Yield is not guaranteed. When interest rates fall, homeowners often rush to refinance their mortgages at lower rates. This means that some of the mortgages in the pool are closed out before all payments have been made to investors. When this occurs, your yield may decline.
- When interest rates rise, the value of your certificate or fund shares may decline.

WHERE TO BUY

- Stockbrokers; mutual funds.

FEES

- Vary depending on the mutual fund.
- With an individual certificate, commission is included in the price. There may be a 1% sales fee.

RISK LEVEL

- Fairly low. The government guarantees that interest and principal will be paid on time each month, but actual yield is not guaranteed. The guarantee protects investors only from default by homeowners.

TAX IMPLICATIONS

- Monthly interest is taxed as ordinary income.
- Monthly principal payments are considered a return of capital and are exempt from taxes.

YOUR INVESTMENT PLANNER FOR GINNIE MAES (GNMAs)

Name of issuer or fund:

Address:

Account number:

Mutual fund name (if any):

Telephone:

Switching fee:

Redemption fee:

Distribution date:

PURCHASES

DATE PURCHASED	# OF SHARES	PRICE/ SHARE	FEE	DIVIDEND REINVEST.	TOTAL $ INCL. FEES	VALUE ON 12/31

SALES

DATE SOLD	# OF SHARES	TOTAL AMOUNT	PROFIT OR LOSS	TAX SITUATION

To keep track of the daily yield, call the Fund's 800 number. For the weekly yield, check the business section of your newspaper for the 7-day average yield. The average monthly yield will appear on the statement you receive.

YIELD			TOTAL RETURN		
Jan _____	May _____	Sep _____	Jan _____	May _____	Sep _____
Feb _____	Je _____	Oct _____	Feb _____	Je _____	Oct _____
Mar _____	Jly _____	Nov _____	Mar _____	Jly _____	Nov _____
Apr _____	Aug _____	Dec _____	Apr _____	Aug _____	Dec _____

See page 54 for helpful formulas.

REAL ESTATE INVESTMENT TRUSTS (REITs)

Real estate investment trusts, or REITs (rhymes with *beets*), are stocks that operate more like mutual funds in that they pool investor dollars to assemble a portfolio of real estate—property and mortgages. They are run by professional managers, have diversified holdings, and pay out dividends and capital gains to shareholders. Since shares trade on the various stock exchanges, you can sell your REIT at any time, a rarity in real estate.

REITs were established by Congress back in the 1960s to give the small investor a means of participating in the benefits of real estate without the headaches traditionally associated with ownership of property. In the 1970s, REITs fell upon hard times and investors lost over $3 billion. Today, new regulations have raised REITs' investment credibility: They are required to keep at least 75% of their assets in real estate, thus reducing management's ability to speculate, and they must distribute 95% of their income to the shareholders.

If you invest in a REIT, you should first find out if it is perpetual or self-liquidating. Perpetual REITs are open-ended and continually buy and sell properties; self-liquidating REITs have a set life span. Properties are held for a given number of years (often 10) and then liquidated. The closer to liquidation date, the higher in price these tend to be since shareholders will be receiving a large chunk of cash from sale of assets.

There are three basic types of REITs:

- EQUITY REITs own portfolios of actual property, such as office buildings, shopping malls, apartment houses. They derive income from both rents and sale of appreciated properties. In 1986, equity REITs appreciated an average of 18% and paid dividends averaging a little over 8%.
- MORTGAGE REITs own portfolios of construction loans and mortgages. They are designed to generate more dividend income than their equity counterparts and are higher in risk. On average they fell 9.3% in price in 1986 but paid impressive dividends: an average of 11.2%.
- HYBRID REITs include both equity and mortgages.

BEST FOR

- Those who want a liquid investment in real estate.
- Small investors who cannot buy investment property.

MINIMUM INVESTMENT

- Price of one share (ideally 100 shares).

PROS

- Potential price appreciation.
- Dividend with competitive yields.
- Participation in commercial real estate.
- Liquidity.
- Indirect hedge against inflation.

CONS

- Price of your shares could fall.
- Demand for property could decline.
- Borrowers could default on mortgages.
- Because REITs must pay out 95% of their earnings, they are more highly leveraged than many stocks.
- Lack traditional tax write-offs associated with owning real estate.

WHERE TO BUY

- Stockbrokers.

FEES

- Standard broker's commission.

RISK LEVEL

- High.

TAX IMPLICATIONS

- Dividends and capital gains taxed as income in year received.

HINTS FOR SELECTING A REIT

Look for a REIT with:
- Consistent dividend growth.
- A strong balance sheet.
- Diversification by type of holding and geographically.
- A small percentage of office buildings (the market is glutted).
- Dividends paid from earnings, not a one-time property sale.
- A low debt-to-equity ratio: 1:1 is the average. (At the height of the trouble in the mid-1970s, it was 4:1.)
- An experienced management team that actively manages the property.
- A proven track record.

Avoid a REIT that:
- Is a blind pool (one that owns very little or no property when issued).
- Owns no property at all.
- Has many vacancies.

YOUR INVESTMENT PLANNER FOR REAL ESTATE INVESTMENT TRUSTS (REITs)

Name of corporation:

Purchased
  through broker:
  with investment club:

Where certificates held:

Stock split?: Yes _____ No _____
  If yes, effective date:
    number shares now owned:
    new price per share:

PURCHASES

DATE PURCHASED	# OF SHARES	PRICE/ SHARE	TOTAL	COMMISSIONS	VALUE ON 12/31

SALES

DATE SOLD	# SHARES SOLD	PRICE/SHARE	$ PROFIT/LOSS

DIVIDEND INCOME

DATE	AMOUNT	DATE	AMOUNT

LIMITED PARTNERSHIPS

A limited partnership is a special type of business structure in which a general partner manages the operation, and limited partners, often thousands, contribute capital by purchasing units in the partnership. The limited partners are passive—they have no say in the day-to-day operation of the partnership and their liability is limited to the amount they invest. The general partner usually has unlimited liability.

In a limited partnership, capital gains, income, and tax benefits flow through to the limited partners. Most partnerships are designed to dispose of their assets within a certain time period and then distribute these proceeds to the shareholders (the limited partners).

Public partnerships have thousands of investors. Units range from $2,000 to $10,000. *Private partnerships* usually have a maximum of 35 partners who contribute anywhere from $10,000 per unit on up to $100,000 and more. Public partnerships, registered with the SEC, provide a prospectus and meet other requirements private partnerships need not meet.

The most popular limited partnerships are real estate limited partnerships (RELPs), which buy property for cash and borrow far less than they did prior to tax reform. These new low- or no-leverage partnerships have less potential for appreciation but generate much more income (8 to 15 or 16%). You can participate for $2,000 to $5,000.

After all taxes, expenses, and the general partner's share have been subtracted from rental income, the remaining income is passed on to the investors. Additional money is distributed in 5 to 10 years, when the partnership sells its holdings.

Tax losses can no longer be used by limited partners to shelter other income, with two exceptions: historic rehabilitations and low-income housing projects.

Before buying, compare returns with those of less risky investments. The likelihood of impressive gains depends primarily on conditions in the real estate market. You may find equal profits with less risk in one of the real estate mutual funds.

BEST FOR

- Those seeking a way to invest in commercial real estate without burdens of direct ownership.
- Those with extra dollars to invest.

MINIMUM INVESTMENT

- *Public partnerships:* $2,000 to $10,000.
- *Private:* $10,000 and up.
- In both cases, you must meet certain income and net worth requirements.

PROS

- Income received from rents.
- Lump sum received when holdings sold.
- Professionally managed.
- Mortgage loan programs have predictable stream of income.

CONS

- Little use as tax shelter.
- Fees high.
- Poor secondary market; since not easy to sell, should be held until liquidated.
- Real estate values and/or rental income could fall.

RISK

- High.
- Dependent upon expertise of general partner.

FEES

- Initial fee, including broker's commission, can run as high as 30% (if higher, don't invest).
- Annual management fees to general partner: 1 to 3% plus up to 10% of net earnings.
- When properties are sold, general partner takes no additional percentage of sale.

TAX IMPLICATIONS

- Income earned is subject to taxes for the most part in the year received.
- Most limited partnerships are no longer tax shelters. Check with your accountant.
- Deductions, when they exist, stem primarily from depreciation and operating expenses and can be used to shelter income that flows in from the project itself. If the deductions are greater than the projects income, then the losses can be used to shelter income from other tax shelters.

KEEP IN MIND

- Before investing, read the prospectus carefully. Find out how experienced the general partner is, exactly how the profits will be divided, and if the general partner has also invested money in the project.
- Then have your accountant or broker review the material. Ask about the loan-to-value ratio, leveraging, occupancy rates, type of property involved and tax benefits.

YOUR INVESTMENT PLANNER FOR LIMITED PARTNERSHIPS

Partnership name: Type of partnership:

Registration number:

Address: General partner's name and address:

Telephone:

Name of broker:

Telephone:

Date purchased: Units purchased: $ Cost/unit: $

Commissions or sales fee: $ Total cost: $

                                                     Where papers located:

DISTRIBUTIONS

DATE	AMOUNT	TOTAL TO DATE	YEAR-END TOTAL

RENTAL REAL ESTATE

Although tax reform reduced some of the breaks of owning rental property, being a landlord is still one of the best of the high-risk investments. You can start small by renting a room, or go big and buy a whole building. Regardless of the size of your investment, you will have an opportunity to earn rental income, cash in on appreciation when and if you sell, and most likely benefit from a handful of tax breaks. A well-run rental property should provide an annual return somewhere between 9 or 10 and 20%.

BEST FOR

- Investors willing to assume the risks associated with real estate.
- Investors with spare cash.
- Those who are handy and can do their own repairs.

MINIMUM INVESTMENT

- Varies with area of the country but plan on minimum of $60,000.

PROS

- Source of steady income from rents.
- Potential price appreciation.
- Certain tax benefits.
- Tends to be a relatively stable investment—people need places to live regardless of the economy.
- Traditionally a hedge against inflation.
- Way to build up equity.

WHAT TO BUY

- Invest in your neighborhood first; it's an area you know. You can keep an eye on your property and if it needs repairs you can either do them yourself or use workers you already know.
- Buy only in desirable areas with low vacancy rates.
- Never buy sight unseen; visit the property in the daytime and at night, during the week and on weekends, and on a rainy day.
- Have the property inspected by a professional engineer and not one recommended by the real estate agent or property owner.
- Check local zoning laws regarding rental property. Know if there are rent control laws that will keep your income down.
- Try to buy from someone anxious to sell. Feel comfortable negotiating; everyone has their price.

CONS

- May be difficult to make a profit; may even produce a loss, especially during first years
- If your income is over $150,000 the tax benefits are sharply reduced.
- Being a landlord is time-consuming; requires a certain temperament.
- Not a very liquid investment.

WHERE TO BUY

- Check newspapers; get to know brokers; talk to bankers about foreclosure sales and tax auctions.

FEES

- Standard real estate brokerage fee when purchasing.
- If someone else manages property, annual management fee can range from 5 to 15% of rental income.
- Down payment and monthly mortgages; real estate taxes; repairs; lawyer's fees.

RISK LEVEL

- High.

TAX IMPLICATIONS

- *If your adjusted gross income is under $150,000, the tax benefits are significant. Deductions can be taken for mortgage interest, property taxes, and part of operating expenses and depreciation. You can also claim deductions in excess of the rental income earned from the property. This is one of the few tax shelters left. You can use these losses, up to a limit of $25,000, to offset your salary and other regular income. The $25,000 of allowable losses is gradually reduced for those whose incomes are between $100,000 and $150,000, so that after $150,000 there are no such benefits. In order to qualify for this break you must actively manage the property, which means playing a role in the day-to-day operations, determining rents, etc.*
- *If your adjusted gross income is above $150,000, income from rental real estate is categorized as a passive activity, and losses can only be used to offset other passive activities, not portfolio income, wages, or salary. A passive activity is one in which someone else takes care of the day-to-day business, supervision, and operations for the investors, as in a limited partnership (see page 44).*

YOUR INVESTMENT PLANNER FOR RENTAL REAL ESTATE

Type of property:

Location of property:

Purchase date:

Purchase price: $

Purchased from:

Co-owners (if any):

Percent of ownership:

Down payment: $

Mortgage held by:

Amount mortgaged: $

Terms of mortgage

   Interest rate:

   Fixed? _____   Variable? _____

   If variable, initial rate good until:

   Lifetime cap:

   Prepayment penalty:

RENTAL INCOME

DATE	AMOUNT	DATE	AMOUNT

DEDUCTIONS

DATE	AMOUNT

PROPERTY TAXES

DATE	AMOUNT

PRECIOUS METALS

Wall Street doom-and-gloomers continually predict the collapse of our economic system or the crash of the market. Even if the worst doesn't occur in your lifetime, you'll see a rise in inflation, perhaps even to double digits, a true recession, or a depression. That's why you might want to put a portion of your portfolio in precious metals—gold, silver, platinum—as a hedge against the future.

There are many ways to invest in precious metals. You can purchase bars directly and take physical possession, storing them in your safe-deposit box or burying them in your backyard. A less cumbersome and more practical arrangement for most people is to purchase a certificate indicating that you own the metal and to let a dealer store the metal for you in a vault.

Coins have no numismatic or collectors' value but are priced based on the value of their content. Among the gold coins are the American Gold Eagle, Canadian Mapleleaf, Australian Nugget, and Chinese Panda. The Silver Eagle is the most popular silver coin; bags of older coins can also be purchased for $1,000 face value. There is even a platinum coin called the Noble.

The riskiest yet potentially most rewarding ways to speculate are through futures and options or through buying shares in one of the precious metals mutual funds or building a portfolio of mining stocks.

Regardless of which approach you take, set aside a small amount, certainly no more than 10% unless you're independently wealthy, to invest in precious metals.

BEST FOR

- Investors seeking a hedge against inflation.

MINIMUM INVESTMENT

- *Coins and bars:* slightly above spot price.
- *Certificates:* $1,000.
- *Commodities contracts:* 6 to 10% of contract's value.
- *Mutual funds:* $1,000.

PROS

- Offers a traditional hedge against inflation.
- Participation in rising prices.

CONS

- Price is extremely volatile.
- Does not yield income.

WHERE TO BUY

- *Coins and bars:* precious metals dealers, coin dealers, larger brokerage firms.
- *Certificates:* precious-metals dealers, major banks, brokerage firms.
- *Commodities contracts:* brokerage firms.
- *Mutual funds:* directly from fund or broker.

FEES

- *Coins and bars:* 3 to 8% above gold content.
- *Certificates:* 2 to 3% commission plus annual storage fee of about 1%.
- *Commodities contracts:* $40 to $50 commission.
- *Mutual funds:* no-load funds have no initial sales charge.

RISK LEVEL

- High.

TAX IMPLICATIONS

- Purchases of coins and bars subject to state and local sales taxes in most states.
- Tax can probably be eliminated if you don't take delivery of the metal but leave it in dealer's vault.
- Profits are considered capital gains and taxed at regular rates.
- Dividends from stocks and mutual funds subject to regular income tax.

YOUR INVESTMENT PLANNER FOR PRECIOUS METALS

Type of metal: Purchased from:

Amount/size: Address:

Price/ounce/share: $ Telephone:

                                                  Commission:

                                                  Total cost:

                                                  Where held:

                                                  Insured?:   Yes _____   No _____

                                                  Appraised value at purchase: $

                                                  Annual storage fees: $

VALUATION/PRICE:	19__	19__	19__
January 1			
March 31			
June 30			
September 30			
December 31			

GOLD MUTUAL FUNDS

Mutual funds (see page 38) offer investors a way to participate in gold without the hassle of holding gold bars or selecting individual mining companies. Because of potential production disruption, the moral issue of apartheid, and other problems in the South African mines, we suggest selecting funds that avoid heavy commitments in that country. Each fund's customer service representatives will explain how much of its portfolio is invested in South Africa. *Note:* Some funds that do not currently invest in South Africa reserve the right to do so at any time. Following are some of the leading gold mutual funds.

FUND
Colonial Advanced Strategies Gold   800-426-3750
Fidelity Select American Gold   800-544-6666
Franklin Gold   800-632-2180
Keystone Precious Metals   800-225-2618
IDS Precious Metals   800-328-8300
United Services New Prospector   800-824-4653
Van Eck Gold Resources   800-221-2220   212-687-5200
Vanguard Gold   800-662-7447

ANNUITIES

An annuity is a form of savings account offered by an insurance company that guarantees regular payments to the purchaser (you) either for a certain time or for life. In return, you make payments (premiums) to the insurance company, either all at once (a *single premium*) or over time (an *installment premium*). An annuity, then, provides income while you're alive, unlike life insurance which provides income to your heirs.

There are two basic types of annuities: fixed and variable. In a *fixed annuity*, the amount you invest (your principal) earns interest at a rate that's guaranteed for a specific time period. It may be as short as 1 year or as long as 5 or 7 years. After the time is up your money is reinvested at the current rate and then guaranteed not to fall below a new minimum. Your principal is guaranteed at all times.

When you take your money out of a fixed annuity on a monthly (or quarterly basis) you receive a guaranteed amount based on your age, sex, and the type of payments you've elected. There is no protection against inflation.

Variable annuities, in contrast, take inflation into account. You, not the insurance company, decide whether to invest your money in stocks, bonds, or money market accounts. Your return, therefore, is variable, fluctuating daily depending upon the performance of the investments. Monthly payments vary too, from one month to the next, based on the value of your account, the amount you put in, and how long you're expected to live. Your principal is not guaranteed. This type of annuity is best for those who follow the market.

You can purchase an annuity long before retirement, known as a deferred annuity, or you can wait until you retire and buy an immediate annuity.

With an *immediate annuity,* your income checks from the insurance company will start appearing in your mailbox soon after purchase, at least within the year. An immediate annuity is often used by people who receive lump sum payments from company pension plans. To set up an immediate payment annuity, you must purchase a single premium annuity.

In a *deferred payment annuity,* no payouts are made until at least a year after purchase and more typically several years after you've paid all premiums. You should buy a deferred annuity only if you know you can leave your money in the plan. It is most suitable for younger people and those who are several years away from retirement.

You can purchase a deferred annuity by a single premium or by continuous installment payments. If you elect to make installment payments, you'll have yet another decision to make: the dollar amounts can be fixed or variable. With the latter, you don't have to pay a specific dollar amount in any one year. With a fixed, you must make annual contributions.

BEST FOR

- Additional source of assured retirement income.
- Investing a lump sum of cash.

MINIMUM INVESTMENT

- *Single premium annuities:* $2,500 or more.
- *Variable premium annuities:* lower minimums, often only $1,000; additional payments may be $100 or more and made at any time.
- *Fixed-premium annuities:* usually $5,000 to $10,000 (minimums).

PROS

- Earn tax-deferred income.
- Forced saving.

CONS

- If you die before payouts begin, income tax must be paid on the profits.
- Tax penalty if you're under age 59½ when withdrawals begin; penalty waived if you're disabled.
- Companies have their own penalties.
- Yields may not be competitive.

WHERE TO BUY

- Insurance brokers and agents, stockbrokers, financial planners, commercial banks, savings & loans, credit unions.

FEES

Vary widely with plan; following are typical:
- Front-end sales charge of 1% to 10%.
- Annual fees of $5 to $30 per year to maximum of 1½% of account value.
- Early withdrawal penalties: 7% declining to zero in 7 years.

RISK LEVEL

- Relatively low if with solid company; select only a company rated A or A+ by A. M. Best & Co.

TAX IMPLICATIONS

- Annuity contributions are not tax deductible.
- Part of monthly payout is return of capital and not taxed; check with insurance company regarding age cutoff for this tax break.
- Cash deposit is not taxed.
- Interest income taxed as ordinary income.

YOUR INVESTMENT PLANNER FOR ANNUITIES

Premium: $ Policy number: _____   Insurance company: _____

Premium type: Variable? _____   Fixed? _____   Agent: _____

Beneficiary: _____   Address: _____

  Address: _____   Telephone: _____

  Telephone: _____

Date payouts begin: _____

Payout period: Monthly? _____   Quarterly? _____   Annually? _____

Premium invested in: _____

Amount received: $ _____

CASH VALUE

DATE	AMOUNT	DATE	AMOUNT

See page 54 for helpful formulas.

SINGLE PREMIUM LIFE INSURANCE

In a single premium life insurance policy you make one lump sum payment (the single premium) of $5,000 or more. This premium then goes two places: most of it into an investment account and the rest to buy life insurance coverage that's roughly 2 to 10 times the dollar amount of your premium payment. Your age and whether or not you smoke are also taken into consideration. The death benefit as well as the cash value of the plan both increase in value over the years.

Single premium life insurance comes in two flavors: whole and variable. In a *single premium whole life* policy, your cash earns interest at a fixed rate for a fixed period of time determined by the insurance company. When the guarantee period is over, the company sets a new rate.

An interesting advantage to SPWL is that you can borrow the earnings made by the cash investment at no cost to you. How? The interest you theoretically pay on the loan is the same as the interest your policy will earn during the time period of the loan. For example, let's say you borrow $10,000 and the insurance company charges 6% for the loan. It then credits your loan account with the 6% your insurance policy earns. This is known as a "wash" in insurance-ese. Thus your true borrowing cost is zero. And you need never pay back the policy loan or pay taxes on the money you borrow.

The key drawbacks you should be aware of are: (1) if you cash out (withdraw all money) of your policy, the earnings will be taxed *unless* you transfer your money to another policy at once; and (2) if you end your policy during the early years, you'll pay a hefty surrender fee: 7 to 9% of the cash value in the first year. This declines to zero in 7 to 10 years.

Single premium variable life is a riskier choice, since the rate of return varies, reflecting the performance of the insurance company's mutual funds. If the funds do well you will probably earn more money than in single premium whole life, where the rate is fixed. Your death benefit is also variable: it rises or falls along with the funds, although it cannot shrink below the amount you initially signed up for.

You can also borrow from a variable policy but there's a fee of 1 to 5% a year.

BEST FOR

- Meeting long-range goals.
- Planning for retirement.
- An IRA alternative.

MINIMUM INVESTMENT

- $5,000 on average.

PROS

- Tax-free earnings accumulation.
- Can borrow from your cash value (up to 90% in some plans) at low rates.
- No tax on buildup unless you surrender policy.
- Death benefit may increase if funds perform well.
- Combines life insurance and savings.
- Entire premium earns interest immediately.
- Can exchange one policy for another without tax consequences (but check carefully to see if you might incur surrender charges).

CONS

- Borrowing against the cash value depletes the death benefit.
- Interest payments on cash value loans are not tax deductible.
- Not a wise short-term investment.
- Not suggested if you just need insurance.
- If you take out all the principal as a loan and fail to make the interest payments, your policy will lapse and all the formerly tax-free earnings will become taxable.
- Initial payment locked in.

WHERE TO BUY

- Insurance companies, insurance agents, stockbrokers, financial planners.

FEES

- Vary widely; check carefully. Ask for the net rate, not the gross rate. This will show the true return on your investment: the amount earned by your cash value minus cost of insurance and administration expenses.
- The spread between the rate the insurance company earns and the rate it credits you with pays the company's expenses and death claims and gives it a profit. In many cases this is about 2 to 2.25%.

TAX IMPLICATIONS

- If you surrender your policy before you die, you will owe income tax on the earnings.
- If you die, the proceeds of your policy pass on to your beneficiary free of income tax.
- If you're collecting social security, loans from your policy are *not* counted when determining how much of your social security check will be taxed.

YOUR INVESTMENT PLANNER FOR SINGLE PREMIUM LIFE INSURANCE

Beneficiary: Insurance company:

  Address: Agent:
                                         Address:

  Telephone:
                                       Telephone:

Date policy purchased:

Premium paid: $

Date payouts begin:

Payout period: Monthly? _____   Quarterly? _____   Yearly? _____

If you can't locate any of the following information in the prospectus, simply call your agent.

Interest rate: %   Premium invested in:

  Guaranteed until: Amount of insurance coverage: $

  Rate tied to:

Early withdrawal penalties

Year 1:	%	Year 3:	%	Year 5:	%
Year 2:	%	Year 4:	%	Year 6:	%

Cash buildup

Year 1: $	Year 6: $	Year 11: $
Year 2: $	Year 7: $	Year 12: $
Year 3: $	Year 8: $	Year 13: $
Year 4: $	Year 9: $	Year 14: $
Year 5: $	Year 10: $	Year 15: $

Loans: If you decide to borrow against your policy, be sure to record the amount borrowed and when you received the money.

Withdrawal of interest earned (does not need to be paid back):
$ (date:)
$ (date:)
$ (date:)
$ (date:)
$ (date:)

From principal/cash value (must be paid back to keep policy valid):
$ (date:)   Interest rate: %
$ (date:)
$ (date:)
$ (date:)
$ (date:)

See page 54 for helpful formulas.

FORMULAS

- *Dividend yield:* $\dfrac{\text{annual dividend per share}}{\text{price of one share}}$

    For example: $\dfrac{\$2}{\$25} = 8\%$

- *P/E ratio:* $\dfrac{\text{price of stock}}{\text{earnings per share}}$

    For example: $\dfrac{\$25}{\$4} = 6.25$

- *Book value:* assets − liabilities − preferred stocks

    For example:

    $$\begin{array}{rl} & \$20 \text{ million in assets} \\ - & 5 \text{ million in liabilities (debt)} \\ - & 1 \text{ million of preferred stock} \\ \hline & 14 \text{ million book value} \end{array}$$

    To convert this to a per share basis, divide by the number of outstanding shares, let's say 2 million.

    $$\dfrac{\$14 \text{ million book value}}{2 \text{ million shares}} = \$7$$

    The book value per share is $7. Most stocks sell above book value.

- *Net asset value* (NAV): Mutual funds compute their assets daily by totaling the current market value of all securities owned by the fund and subtracting all the liabilities. The balance is divided by the number of shares outstanding. This number is given as a dollar amount in the newspaper.

WHICH BANK YIELD IS BEST?

In order to figure out which bank is offering the best deal in terms of interest, you can use the following formula:

minimum deposit × interest rate

$$= \text{annual interest income}$$

For example: $\$2,500 \times 8\% = \$200$.

Then simply multiply the monthly service charge by 12:

$$\$4 \times 12 = \$48$$

Subtract this amount from the annual interest income:

$$\$200 - \$48 = \$152$$

Divide

$$\$152 \text{ by } \$2,500 = 6.1\%$$

This is the actual yield.

SIMPLE INTEREST

The dollar cost of borrowing money is based on three things: the amount borrowed (the principal), the rate of interest, and the amount of time. To find simple interest, use this formula:

$$\text{interest} = \text{principal} \times \text{interest rate} \times \text{time}$$

Interest rate is a ratio. For instance, an interest rate of 10% means 10 for every 100, or 10 to 100, or 10 divided by 100. When interest is expressed as a decimal, two decimal places equal the percent sign. Therefore, 10% becomes 0.10, or ten one-hundreths (10/100).

FINDING INTEREST RATE ON A LOAN

Say you borrow $1,000 at 10% and repay it in a lump sum at the end of a year. To find the amount of interest on the loan, you can use the formula given above (but often expressed by these abbreviations):

$$I = P \times R \times T$$

$$I = \$1,000 \times 0.10 \times 1$$

The answer is $100.

To figure the total amount due on the loan in 2 years:

$$\text{total amount due} = P + (P \times R \times T)$$

$$= \$1,000 + (\$1,000 \times 0.10 \times 2)$$

$$= \$1,000 + \$200$$

$$= \$1,200$$

REFINANCING YOUR MORTGAGE

The rule of thumb is: Don't refinance unless there's at least a 2-percentage-point difference between the old and new mortgage rates; otherwise you won't recoup the expenses of taking out a new loan. If you're moving within 2 years, don't refinance regardless of rates.

PART THREE

THROUGH THE FINANCIAL MAZE

It isn't easy to find the right investment advisor; it's even more difficult to change if one doesn't work out. And once you do settle on a broker, banker, or mutual fund, that's only the beginning. You'll soon face a barrage of statements, confirmation slips, papers to sign, choices to make.

This section walks you through the financial maze. It helps you select a broker, open and use an account, and unravel the various statements you receive. You'll learn what questions to ask, when, and how; what the guidelines are for getting your broker's attention; what to do if you're a small investor.

If you need special hand-holding or if you become exasperated or worried and wonder who to turn to for help, then refer back to the list below. It too will help.

WHEN YOU NEED SOMEONE TO HOLD YOUR HAND

These organizations provide material and advice for the general investor.

- Institute of Certified Financial Planners
  Two Denver Highlands
  10065 East Harvard Avenue, Suite 320
  Denver, CO 80231
  303-751-7600

- International Association for Financial Planning
  2 Concourse Parkway, Suite 800
  Atlanta, GA 30328
  800-241-2148 (outside Georgia)
  404-395-1605

- Consumer Affairs Specialist
  Federal Reserve System
  20th and C Streets, NW
  Washington, DC 20551
  202-452-3000

- Bankcard Holders of America
  (lists banks with low rates on credit cards)
  333 Pennsylvania Avenue, SE
  Washington, DC 20003
  800-638-6407
  202-543-5805 (in Washington)

- Investment Company Institute
  (trade association for mutual funds)
  1600 M Street, NW
  Washington, DC 20036
  202-293-7700

- American Association of Individual Investors
  612 North Michigan Avenue
  Chicago, IL 60611
  312-280-0170

- Office of Consumer Affairs
  The Securities and Exchange Commission
  450 Fifth Street, NW
  Washington, DC 20549
  202-272-7440
  202-272-3100 (for the hearing impaired)

- SIPC (Securities Investor Protection Corp.)
  900 17th Street, NW
  Washington, DC 20006
  202-223-8400

- National Insurance Consumer Organization
  121 North Payne Street
  Alexandria, VA 22314
  703-549-8050

- American Association of Certified Appraisers
  800 Compton Road
  Cincinnati, OH 45231
  800-543-2222
  513-729-1400

CHOOSING AND USING FULL-SERVICE BROKERS

October. This is one of the peculiarly dangerous months to speculate in stocks. The others are July, January, September, April, November, May, March, June, December, August, and February.

—*Mark Twain*

But not if you read this book and use a smart stockbroker. The perfect broker of course, just like a perfect child or spouse, is somewhat elusive, but you can increase your chances for a successful union if you use a little common sense and a lot of assertiveness.

FINDING THE BEST

First of all, don't rush the process. Go about selecting a stockbroker as you would a doctor, dentist, or any other member of your personal professional team. Ask friends and colleagues whose opinions you respect for names. Find out who your lawyer and accountant use.

Then, take time to interview at least three candidates *in person*. Beforehand, draw up a list of questions (see box); bring it with you and don't trust your memory, jot down the answers. Later on compare each broker's responses.

When interviewing brokers, be prepared to answer their questions too. They will want to know how much you have to invest, what your income and net worth are, as well as your investment goals. Then ask each one to tell you how they would invest $5,000 or $10,000 of your money—in broad terms; for example, 50% in stocks, 20% in municipal bonds, 10% in a money market fund, 7% in T-bills, 7% in precious metals, and 6% in a RELP.

The five key things to find out about a broker are: experience, training, trustworthiness, track record, and references.

After the interviews, check the references, review your notes, and pay attention to your instincts. This person will be responsible for charting your financial future, so you want someone you like, can trust, and who knows how to make money in bull as well as in bear markets. Which leads to the final point: never hire a broker who seems to be having a financial struggle. If they can't make money for themselves, they certainly can't make it for you!

HOW TO GET YOUR BROKER'S ATTENTION

If you feel your broker is ignoring you or in some way not meeting your expectations, don't avoid the issue. Talk to your broker about it; try to change the situation; and if you can't, change brokers. But before you do:

- Realize that a good broker *should be* busy and pressed for time.
- Try to call your broker either before or after the market closes.
- Compliment your broker when he or she picks a winner.
- Say you'd like to *review* your portfolio, at your broker's convenience.
- Don't call continually just for quotes, unless you're continually trading.
- Place your orders quickly: know what you want and how much.
- Do your own homework; don't plead being a financial dummy.
- Take your broker to dinner.

But, alas, if indeed you've made a mistake, and your broker is losing your money, then by all means find another. Cut your losses, but cut them politely. You may need your old broker's help in the future, perhaps to retrieve an old record or to help with a tax problem—or you may run into them at the ninth hole or in your community theater on Saturday evening.

QUESTIONS TO ASK BROKER CANDIDATES

1 How long have you been a broker?
2 Where did you receive your training?
3 Where do you get your investment ideas; how do you pick stocks?
4 What do you do when a stock drops in price? When do you sell? How do you decide?
5 What is your success ratio? How does that compare with the S&P 500?
6 Do you consult with clients before buying securities?
7 How do you feel about working with a client like me who is: inexperienced, wealthy, not wealthy, young, retired, cautious, etc.?
8 Will you give me the names of three clients as references?
9 What is the most speculative investment you recommend?
10 How do you correct your mistakes?

YOU SHOULD NOT HIRE A BROKER WHO

- Refuses to provide references.
- Seems too fast-paced for you.
- Makes you uncomfortable.
- Is too busy to return your calls.
- Tells you to put all your money in one "hot" stock.
- Promises to make you rich.

CHOOSING AND USING DISCOUNT BROKERS

You probably associate May Day with the rites of spring, blooming jonquils, and general frivolity over the impending warm weather. True, but it's also a landmark day in the brokerage business: it marks the birthday of the discount broker.

On May 1, 1975, the SEC removed the price floor from commissions, thus bringing to a close the era of the fixed-rate system and opening the door for negotiation. Up until that time, everyone, regardless of the size of their portfolio, was forced to use a full-service broker, such as Merrill Lynch, E. F. Hutton, Smith Barney, or Prudential-Bache. Today, discount brokers, who sell securities at rates 30 to 80% below those of full-service firms, make up nearly 25% of the business.

A discount firm is essentially a no-frills operation where your buy and sell orders are executed at low rates and where portfolio management, research, and market advice are almost nonexistent. This type of firm is ideal for certain investors, in particular those who enjoy doing their own research, selecting their own stocks, and making their own buy and sell decisions.

If you're a novice or need a lot of hand-holding, you're better off with the many types of support offered by a full-service firm. The only exception might be if you have inherited 100 shares of a stock and you merely wish to sell it—then using a discounter makes good economic sense.

How can discount firms charge so much less? It's simple: they do less. These firms offer streamlined service, have low overhead, pay their staff salaries rather than commissions, and do not support a team of analysts, specialists, researchers, writers, etc.

SELECTING THE BEST DISCOUNT FIRM

Many of the larger, well-established discount firms advertise in the financial pages of newspapers and magazines. Although this is a good place to begin your search, you should also ask friends about firms they use and are pleased with. There's no particular need to interview a discount broker since it's *you* who will manage your portfolio. However, if it's convenient you may want to visit the offices of one or two to add to your overall impression.

- Study the literature of several firms; compare commission rates. Note the different minimums and any extras the firm offers.
- Call several firms at various times of the day. At least 90% of your contact with a discounter is on the phone. You want to use a firm with plenty of operators and people to place your orders. Time is money—the market can move 2 points while you're waiting for the muzak to end.

- Check with your bank; many offer a discount service through a subsidiary.
- Ask each firm several questions, to judge the quality of the firm as much as to find out the answers:
1 Do you automatically sweep unused cash into a money market fund? Which one? Are there check-writing privileges?
2 Do you sell bonds? Options?
3 Can I trade with you through my home computer?
4 Do you have a newsletter? Any research?
5 May I see a sample monthly statement?
6 Are you a member of SIPC? How much is my account insured for?
7 How long have you been in business?
8 Can I open my IRA or Keogh plan with you?

When using a discount firm you must know what type of order to place, since you will not have a regular broker to advise you.

- A *market order* is an order to buy or sell at once at the current market price. The price is not guaranteed but execution usually takes place immediately.
- In a *limit order* you decide in advance at what price you want to trade, stating that you're not willing to trade beyond this limit. If your price limit is not reached, there's no sale or purchase, which means you could miss out on a rise in price.
- A *stop order* specifies at what price you will sell. This is a suspended order and goes into effect only if the stock touches the stated price. Use it to sell your stock after it reaches a certain price below the current market price and thus to protect yourself from large losses. A *stop order to sell* is placed at a price below the current market price. A *stop order to buy* is placed at a price above the current market price.

Any of these orders can be given for a certain time period: an *open order* stays active until filled or cancelled, a *day order* for one day.

USE A DISCOUNT BROKER IF

- You trade on a regular basis—two or three times a month.
- You want to make a one-time sale of a stock or bond.
- You want to get your feet wet in the market.
- You have confidence in your own research.
- You don't panic at having made a mistake.
- You are a member of an investment club.

OPENING AN ACCOUNT

Once you've selected a broker, your next step is opening an account. You'll be asked to provide sufficient information so the broker meets the requirements of New York Stock Exchange Rule 405, the "know thy customer" rule. The amount of information varies from firm to firm, but generally you can expect to be asked:

Name
Address
Social security number
Telephone
Employer's name and address
Personal references
How referred to firm
Citizenship
Proof of legal age if you're young
Spouse's name
Spouse's employer's name and address
Banks
Previous brokerage accounts
Other extant brokerage accounts

If you're going to trade options, you'll be asked your income, net worth, and experience in investing. You must also acknowledge receipt of a special Options Clearing Corporation prospectus and sign an options agreement.

When you open an account, your broker will ask if you want the securities held with the firm (*in street name*) or registered in your name and sent to you. If you decide to take physical possession, it will take several weeks for them to arrive after a trade. If you leave them in street name, it will be as a computer entry. Your dividends and stock splits will be automatically collected for you.

When securities are registered in your name, you receive all the company's reports and dividends. Should you change your address, you must notify the transfer agent of all the companies in which you own shares. The name of the transfer agent is on the certificate; it's frequently a bank.

TYPES OF ACCOUNTS

There are two basic types of accounts—cash and margin. By far the most common is the *cash account* in which you may buy and sell securities as long as you pay within 5 business days after the transaction.

A *margin account* allows you to borrow to buy securities. You must sign a special loan consent, which pledges your stocks as collateral and grants the broker permission to lend your margined stock to others. Your stocks must be held in street name in a margin account because they are collateral for the unpaid or margined portion of your account. The New York Stock Exchange requires a minimum initial equity of $2,000 for a margin account.

The Federal Reserve Board currently requires that you pay cash for 50% of margin purchases, so if you buy $5,000 worth of stock you must pay $2,500 in cash. The rest is debited to your account and subject to interest. The interest may fluctuate depending upon other interest rates and the size of your account.

If your equity falls below a certain minimum, due to a decline in the market, you are subject to a *margin call,* and you must put up additional money or marginable securities at once.

A margin account is suitable only for experienced investors.

A *discretionary account* requires written authorization on your part plus approval by an officer or partner of the brokerage house. Essentially you are signing a power of attorney, allowing the broker to buy and sell without consulting you first. If your broker is trustworthy and smart, you will be getting free money management in a discretionary account. However, it can lead to many problems, and customers often feel, rightly or wrongly, that the broker is "churning" their account, or doing trades in order to create commissions. Open a discretionary account only with the greatest discretion!

A *Uniform-Gift-to-Minors* account can be set up for children. The parent, grandparent, or whoever establishes the account names a custodian for the minor (you may name yourself). All activity is then executed by the adult for the child. The custodian can make whatever decisions seem wise and in the best interests of the child. When the child reaches majority he or she takes over the account.

A *joint account* can be opened by any two individuals, whether or not they live in wedded bliss. The most common is *joint tenancy with rights of survivorship.* If one dies, the other then receives all the property in the account. Because it bypasses probate and goes directly to the survivor, this is known as the "poor man's will."

You may also have a *tenancy in common* in which the survivor receives none of the deceased's share of the account. Instead, it goes to the deceased's heirs and the survivor must open a new account.

Check with your lawyer before opening any type of joint account.

QUESTIONS TO ASK YOUR BROKER

How safe is my brokerage account?
You should only open an account with a firm that is a member of SIPC (Securities Investor Protection Corp.), a nonprofit corporation that protects the customers of registered securities dealers if a firm is financially unable to meet its obligations. SIPC is funded by members and is not a federal agency.

Each customer account is covered for up to $100,000 in cash and up to $400,000 worth of securities, such as stocks, bonds, notes, and certain CDs. SIPC does *not* cover unregistered investment contracts, gold, silver, or any type of commodity or commodity option.

Is my money market fund covered by SIPC?
Shares of money market funds are regarded as securities, not cash, if in a mutual fund. Therefore, they are protected just like any other security. But remember, SIPC does *not* protect you against declines in the market value of mutual funds, stocks, or bonds.

How do I sell stocks I have in my safe-deposit box?
If you sell a security that's in your name, not in street name, you have two choices: (1) Sign your name on the back of the stock certificate precisely as it is on the front, including any initials. If it's registered in joint names, you and your co-owner must both sign. However, it's best not to sign a stock certificate until you're in your broker's office. (2) Sign a stock power form, which you can get from the brokerage firm or from most banks. It's a substitute for the signature portion of the stock certificate, so when using a stock power you don't also have to sign the certificate. A stock power can be mailed separately from the certificate, which protects you should the certificate be lost in the mail.

Should I pay attention to what exchange a stock trades on?
As you can see by the table below, the companies accepted for listing on the New York Stock Exchange (NYSE) are larger. However, many equally solid companies trade on the American (AMEX)—they may be newer, smaller, or simply prefer the AMEX. The exchange is not a major consideration, but the company's balance sheet and fundamentals certainly are.

REQUIREMENTS TO BE LISTED ON DIFFERENT EXCHANGES

	NYSE	AMEX
Number of stockholders	2,000	1,000
Number of shares publicly held	1,100,000	500,000
Market value of these shares	$18,000,000	$3,000,000
Tangible assets	$16,000,000	$4,000,000
Pretax income latest year	$ 2,500,000	$ 750,000

What are institutional investors?
These are banks, insurance companies, pension plans, trusts, etc. They often influence the direction of the market because they trade in such huge quantities. Frequently, over 70% of the buying and selling done on the New York Stock Exchange in one day is done by the institutions. On the American and OTC it is often 25% or more.

What is a point?
- *When referring to stocks,* a point is $1. So if Clorox moves up 3 points, it's gone up $3 a share.
- *When referring to bonds,* a point means $10, because a bond is quoted as a percentage of $1,000. Therefore, a bond that moves up 3 points actually increases 3% of $1,000, or $30, in value. If you read or hear that a bond advanced from 90 to 94, it indicates a dollar advance from $900 to $940.
- *When referring to market averages,* a point is just a point: if the S&P 500 moves from 330 to 333, it simply moves up 3 points. With indexes, a point does not mean $1.

BROKERAGE ACCOUNTS

Once you've completed the interview process and settled on a broker you feel you can work with, use the space below to jot down some information. Be sure to keep this record current if you change brokers.

Name of firm:
Address:
Account #:
Name of account holder:
Trustee:
Location of statements:

Broker:
Telephone:

Address:

Commission rates:
Discount:

INVESTMENT CLUBS

Stocks, Supper, and Socializing; Investing, Ingesting, and Interacting: unbeatable combinations are offered by participation in an investment club. The facts speak for themselves: although most clubs are initially inexperienced when it comes to the stock market, after 3 to 5 years they generally outperform the market. A recent study of National Association of Investment Clubs member portfolios revealed that since 1960 the average portfolio has earned more than the S&P 500 Index in all but 6 years.

Investment clubs are small groups of people, usually 10 to 20, who pool their money, do their own research, exchange ideas, and invest together in the stock market. Most meet once a month. It is not necessary to be knowledgeable about stocks to start a club—the idea is to learn together with friends. Clubs are ideal for those with limited cash and little expertise, although sophisticated, Jaguar-driving, diamond-studded types also have built their fortunes through being club members.

The National Association of Investment Clubs (NAIC) has 7,000 club members and approximately 100,000 individual members. This nonprofit organization provides a plethora of educational materials, stock ideas, and guidelines for running a successful club.

The NAIC investment philosophy is extremely sound, if not wildly innovative. The basic tenets are:

- Invest a fixed monthly amount regardless of how the market is performing. This gives members the advantage of dollar cost averaging (see below) in which more shares of stock are purchased at lower prices and fewer at higher prices.
- Reinvest all earnings in order to achieve the advantage of compounding.
- Invest in growth companies whose sales and earnings are already increasing faster than their industry group and/or the overall economy.
- Diversify your investments. The NAIC suggests that a club's portfolio be divided as follows: 25% in leading companies in the major growth industries; 25% in smaller companies that are riskier but have a higher growth rate, and the remaining 50% in solid blue chip stocks.

The aim of every investment club is to double its investments every 5 years—and most succeed.

HOW TO START AN INVESTMENT CLUB

If you're unable to find an existing club to join (try your YMCA, YWCA, adult education center, church, or synagogue), then hesitate not: start your own.

Contact the NAIC (address below) for a free copy of "Suggested Steps for Starting an Investment Club" to read prior to the first meeting.

STEP 1 Get 15 to 20 people with like interests together—try work, tennis club, PTA, or neighborhood association. You do not need to find all the members yourself: talk to two or three friends and ask them to enlist several more. If your co-workers form the nucleus of your group, keep them to half your membership: variety is as important as compatibility.

STEP 2 At your first meeting, elect officers, decide which evening you will meet, discuss an investment philosophy, and establish a dollar amount to invest monthly (the average of existing clubs is $44 per person). You'll find it works best if everyone invests the same amount.

STEP 3 Assign specific research responsibilities. Each member is expected to do regular independent stock research and report findings to the group. The group then votes on whether to buy or sell.

STEP 4 Select a broker, ideally one known to members, who has worked with clubs before. Included in your NAIC membership is a $25,000 fidelity bond from Aetna Casualty and Surety Co., which protects club members against fraud and dishonesty.

STEP 5 Select a name for the club.

More detailed guidelines are available from:

National Association of Investment Clubs
1515 East Eleven Mile Road
Royal Oak, MI 48067
313-543-0612

Annual membership is $30; a subscription to *Better Investing* is $15.

Membership, which is open to both individuals and clubs, includes a number of excellent publications including *The Investor's Manual, Stock Selection Guide and Report,* and *Better Investing Magazine.* As a member, you also have access to detailed reports on selected corporations, stock charts, portfolio management ideas, and record-keeping materials.

DOLLAR COST AVERAGING

By using this simple formula you wind up buying more shares of a stock or mutual fund at low prices than at high prices. You invest a fixed dollar amount, say $100 every month, *no matter whether the market goes up or down.* When prices are up, your $100 will buy fewer shares; when prices drop, it will buy more.

Dollar cost averaging is most easily done through a mutual fund, since commissions eat into profits on small trades of individual stocks. Each fund sets its own minimum requirements and subsequent contributions.

TIME DURING WHICH YOU MAKE DEPOSITS AT $25 PER MONTH	ADDITIONAL AMOUNT DEPOSITED IN PERIOD INDICATED AT $25 PER MONTH	DIVIDENDS RECEIVED IN PERIOD AT $1.20/ SHARE/YEAR	SUM ON HAND TO PURCHASE SHARES AT QUARTERLY PURCHASE DATE	NUMBER OF SHARES BOUGHT THIS PERIOD	TOTAL SHARES OWNED AT END OF PERIOD
End of first 3 months	$ 75	$ 0.000	$ 75.00	3.750	3.750
End of second 3 months	75	1.125	76.12	3.806	7.556
End of third 3 months	75	2.267	77.26	3.863	11.419
End of first year	75	3.426	78.42	3.921	15.340
Year 2	300	25.646	325.64	16.283	31.623
Years 3–5	900	201.812	1101.81	55.091	86.714
Years 6–10	1500	835.829	2335.82	116.793	203.507

Different results would be achieved if the price of the stock went up or down or the dividends were raised or lowered. You can invest more than $25 a month and in more than one company if you wish.
Source: NAIC

DIVIDEND REINVESTMENT PLANS

The simplest way to add to your stock portfolio is through automatic dividend reinvestment, a plan offered by over 1,000 corporations to their shareholders. Many of these are solid blue chip companies or public utilities.

Under these plans, instead of collecting your dividend every quarter, you authorize the company to reinvest your dividends in additional shares of stock. You not only increase your holdings painlessly and effortlessly, you avoid broker's commissions, and some companies offer a 3 to 5% discount on the price of the new shares.

Dividends that are reinvested are taxable as income just as if you had received cash, however. And if the new dividends are purchased at a discount from the going market price, the discounted amount is taxed too—based on the market price as of the dividend payment date.

Some companies also allow shareholders to make cash payments into the plan in order to fatten their accounts. McDonald's Corporation, for example, permits cash contributions of up to $3,000 per quarter.

For a list of companies offering dividend reinvestment plans, send $2 to:

Public Relations
Standard & Poor's Corp.
25 Broadway
New York, NY 10004

If you're interested, contact the company at once, since it often takes several months to activate the plan. Participation generally starts with the next dividend payment *if* your request is received and processed prior to the dividend record date. This date, when the company records the dividend in its books, is 15–45 days prior to the actual payment of the dividend.

RATIO PLANS

Ratio plans are based on the premise that if you spread out your buying and selling over the ups and down of the market you will make profits in the long run. Their purpose is to take the guesswork out of spotting the turns in the market.

In the *constant dollar ratio plan*, you buy and sell to maintain the dollar value of your stock holdings. For example, if you buy $5,000 worth of shares in a growth mutual fund and it appreciates to $6,000 in several months, then you must sell $1,000 worth of shares in order to maintain the constant dollar value of $5,000. If, on the other hand, the shares fall to $4,000, you buy $1,000 worth to bring your holdings back up to $5,000.

In the *constant ratio plan*, you buy and sell to maintain the ratio between different types of securities, such as $5,000 worth of stocks and $2,500 worth of bonds for a 2:1 ratio. When the market rises or falls, you then buy or sell shares accordingly.

SPECIAL INFORMATION FOR SMALL INVESTORS

Surprise! You don't have to have $5,000 or even $500 to begin building a portfolio of stocks. There are several investment programs especially designed for the small investor. They're so effective, in fact, that large numbers of big investors use them, too.

THE BLUEPRINT℠ PROGRAM

This plan, currently offered only by Merrill Lynch, provides an inexpensive and easy way to buy both stocks and precious metals. Your initial investment must be $100 for both stocks and gold or silver (because of the higher risk associated with precious metals, Merrill Lynch suggests you invest no more than 15% of your portfolio in this area). Subsequent minimum purchase is only $50.

Because you're investing by the dollar amount rather than by numbers of shares, you can purchase fractional shares or ounces of these investments.

Merrill Lynch gives you another break: commissions are as much as 40% off the firm's regular charges for trades under $5,000. The upper limit per transaction is $5,000.

The firm mails lists of recommended stocks to participants in the plan. These securities are selected for long-term growth and above-average yields. And, as an additional service, you can buy and sell, receive stock recommendations, and check on the status of your account by phone. For details, call 800-221-2856.

LOW COST INVESTMENT PLAN

Another way to buy small amounts of stocks is through the unique Low Cost Investment Plan sponsored by the National Association of Investment Clubs (NAIC).

NAIC has joined the dividend reinvestment programs of a number of corporations. As a member of NAIC, you can deposit money in these plans by sending a check to the association, where it is held in an escrow account until the company's dividend investment date, at which time NAIC purchases the shares. These shares are then transferred into your individual account. After that, you can send future payments directly to the corporation.

NAIC charges a one-time fee of $5 for each stock you wish to buy, far lower than even a discount broker's commission. Although you can join the dividend reinvestment plan of any corporation that offers one, NAIC's plan is less costly and can save time—you sidestep brokerage commissions. Through this plan you can also buy just one share if you like, something that's far too costly to do through a stockbroker.

Companies participating in the NAIC's Low Cost Investment Program are:

Aetna Life & Casualty
American Family Corp.
Armco, Inc.
Ashland Oil
Avery International
Brown-Forman
Century Maine Power
Dana Corp.
Day International
Disney (Walt)
Dow Chemical Co.
Federal-Mogul
Foxboro Co.
General Signal
Gerber Products
W. R. Grace
Hannaford Brothers
Harsco Corp.
HCA
Iowa Resources
Kellogg Co.
McDonald's Corp.
NBD Bancorp
Primark Corp.
Public Serv. Co. of Colorado
Quaker Oats
RPM, Inc.
St. Paul Companies

PAINLESS WAYS TO SAVE

STOCK PURCHASE PLANS   Your employer, surprisingly, is often a viable savings alternative to your bank or stockbroker. That's because many corporations offer employees an inexpensive way to buy individual shares of their stock. These shares are usually offered at a discount—as much as 15% off the price the general public must pay. In addition, you avoid paying any stockbroker's commission.

Companies offer stock purchase plans not entirely out of the goodness of their hearts, but in order to encourage you to work harder and develop a vested interest in the firm's profitability. However, there are also many advantages for you as well.

PROTECT YOUR RIGHTS

T. Boone Pickens has started a shareholders association to lobby for small shareholders' interests. Details: United Shareholders Association, 1667 K Street, NW, Washington, DC 20006; 202-393-4600. Annual dues: $50.

Plans vary, but typically you can invest anywhere from 1 to 10% of your salary each year in a stock purchase plan. Once you designate the percentage you wish to invest in the plan it usually cannot be changed during that year, but check with your personnel office for specific rulings.

Most companies will automatically deduct the amount you designate from your paycheck. These dollars are placed in a special interest-bearing account and at specified times (generally once a year), shares of the company's stock will be purchased in your name.

In most plans, participants can purchase shares at the lower of two prices: (1) the price the day the employee option to sign up for the plan was given, or (2) the price the day the stock is actually purchased.

The employee discount, the low purchase price, and the absence of a broker's fee mean you receive a greater return on your stock than if you purchased the same number of shares in the traditional fashion. Even if you decide to sell them immediately, you can lock in a profit based on the discount price minus any sales commission.

Remember, however, never put all your eggs in one basket. If your company falls on hard times or if the stock market takes a dive, you don't want all your savings tied up in an issue that's likely to drop in price. So, follow the same sound investment principles in purchasing your company's stock as you would with any other issue.

THREE LOW-MINIMUM MONEY MARKET MUTUAL FUNDS
Most mutual funds require minimum investments of at least $1,000. However, there are a handful that cater to investors with less than that amount to start with. Call each of the following funds, check the current yields, and ask for a copy of the prospectus before investing. (See pages 22–23 for more on money market mutual funds.)

Franklin Money Fund	$500 minimum	800-632-2180
Liberty Money Market Trust	$500 minimum	800-245-4770 412-392-6300
Oppenheimer Asset Builder Program (must agree to have a minimum of $25 per month taken from your checking account and deposited into the fund)		800-525-9310

AUTOMATIC PAYROLL DEDUCTION PLANS   The easiest way for most of us to save is to never let our fingers actually touch money. You can arrange for this if there is an automatic payroll deduction plan where you work.

Have a set amount deducted from each paycheck and transferred automatically into a money market fund, a savings plan, or even to buy EE Savings Bonds (see page 14).

If your company does not offer this plan, talk to your bank. Most will deduct money from your checking account on a predetermined day of the month, and transfer the money into the bank's money market deposit account or savings account.

CREDIT UNIONS   These nonprofit cooperative financial institutions are owned by their members, who are also the borrowers and savers. They typically offer higher yields, lower fees, and more favorable loan rates than commercial banks. Credit unions are sponsored by large businesses, churches, and professional and civic associations. The basic requirement for participation is that you work for the sponsoring company or be affiliated with the sponsoring organization or group. Because they are nonprofit, their savings or would-be profits are passed on to members in the form of higher interest rates and lower loan rates. Over 52 million Americans now use their credit union for basic financial services.

Credit unions offer a variety of services, including savings and checking accounts, discount stockbrokers, and money market accounts. Many also offer credit cards at rates 3 to 5% lower than those sponsored by banks and with no annual fee. Some also have first mortgages and automated teller machine service. Nearly every credit union participates in an automatic payroll deduction plan.

You can open a "share" account (the credit union term for savings account) for very little—$5 to $50. Interest-bearing checking accounts, called "share drafts," and money market accounts both offer extremely favorable terms. Because the staff at a credit union is dealing directly with a person who belongs to the organization, service tends to be friendlier. It's often easier to borrow money than at a large bank where you are a stranger.

There are approximately 10,000 credit unions and 5,000 chartered unions, all of which are federally insured. A smaller number are privately insured. If you join a credit union, make certain your account is federally insured up to $100,000 per depositor.

Check at where you work, the telephone book, and your Better Business Bureau for a credit union in your area. You can also contact the Credit Union National Association, P.O. Box 431, Madison, WI 53701. They will put you in touch with credit unions in your area and send you several brochures explaining how credit unions work and how to join one or organize one yourself.

READING YOUR BROKERAGE FIRM STATEMENT

Harry Truman must have been reading his brokerage firm's statement when he said, "If you can't convince them, confuse them!"

Every firm, whether it's full service or discount, mails out monthly statements that have confusing ingredients. How confusing depends on the firm—and you. If you're willing to spend a little study time you'll conquer it; if not you'll be among those who never read their statements. Regardless of whether you read them or not, always save them—for tax purposes, to catch mistakes, and as a record of your portfolio.

The explanations below will help you interpret your statement in a general way. But if you need answers to specific questions, don't hesitate to call your broker. (Try to confine such calls to before and after market hours, when your broker's life is less hectic.) When you get the answers, jot them down and clip them to your file. One sure way to alienate your broker is to ask the same question month after month.

HOW TO READ A SAMPLE STATEMENT

On the right is a typical brokerage firm statement. Note that the broker's name is listed under the heading Account Executive.

Section 1 is the Financial Summary of the whole account for the month. This lists the value of all "securities," which include cash (called "net money balance") and the securities portfolio. Note on the far right the phrase Real Fund Dividends. This is the brokerage firm's money market fund. It is included in the Financial Summary.

Section 2, Account Activity, explains what transactions occurred—all buy and sell orders. It includes the .26 opening balance of cash, plus dividends earned. On July 21 the broker purchased 3 calls on Chrysler Corp.'s October 35s, which expire on October 17, for $4.50 each. They were purchased for a total investment of $1,407.54. The trade took place on the CBOE (Chicago Board of Options Exchange). To pay for this purchase, $1,407 worth of Real Fund was sold on July 22.

Section 3 covers LFR (L. F. Rothschild) mutual fund activity for this month. Note that $1,407 was used for the purchase of the Chrysler calls. In addition, the money fund earned dividend income of $28.75.

Section 4 covers Security Positions, a list of the number and current value of the stocks and bonds held in the account as of July 31. Over on the left, the word *cash* indicates they were purchased for cash and not on margin. If they were in a margin account it would read *margin*.

This account has among its holdings 200 shares of Holiday Corp. We don't know at what price they were purchased, but at the date of this statement they were worth $32 per share for a total value of $6,400.00. The grand total of all securities in the account, including the money fund, was $16,408.50.

This statement is relatively easy to follow, although it assumes a certain amount of knowledge. Note that it does not indicate which transactions the IRS will be notified of, as does the E. F. Hutton statement on page 69.

OTHER USES FOR YOUR MONTHLY STATEMENT

- If you save each monthly statement you will have a running documentation of the net value of your brokerage account. If it remains steady or increases then you and your broker are doing well; if on the other hand the net value posts continual declines, you must re-evaluate your broker's decisions in light of current market conditions and consider changing your financial advisor.

- Your statement records the amount of income produced by each security along with its estimated annual income. This information is useful in determining how much income you are earning from your individual securities.

- Your trading history—i.e., capital gains and losses—is also documented.

- The December 31 statement provides the total annual income, one of the most useful documents in preparing your income tax.

In addition to these uses, your statement also tells you when your account is getting close to being undermargined, i.e., has shrunk to such an extent that you must add additional money or equities to bring it up to acceptable levels. Being undermargined seldom concerns margin account investors in a stable or rising stock market, but in a falling market margin calls grow in number. You can avoid a margin call, or liquidation of your account, by careful reading of your statement.

The New York Stock Exchange requires that your margin equity be at least 25% of the value of the securities held in your account, and certain brokerage firms often have higher requirements, typically 30%. To determine how close your account is to a margin call, take the *net portfolio value* and divide it by the *net market value of priced securities* to determine the percentage. These figures are provided in the part of the statement under the heading "Financial Summary."

IN ACCOUNT WITH

L.F. ROTHSCHILD, UNTERBERG, TOWBIN, INC.
55 WATER ST., NEW YORK, NEW YORK 10041
MEMBERS ALL LEADING EXCHANGES

BUSINESS INTRODUCED BY
SILBERBERG, ROSENTHAL & CO.
522 FIFTH AVENUE
NEW YORK, NEW YORK 10036

JOHN A. SMITH

100 MAIN STREET

HOMETOWN, NY 00000

ACCOUNT NO.	SOCIAL SEC/I.D. NO.	STATEMENT PERIOD FROM	THROUGH		ACCOUNT EXECUTIVE	TELEPHONE NO.	PAGE
00-1234	123-45-6789	07/01/87	07/31/87	00-00	JONES, NELSON	212-123-4567	1

FINANCIAL SUMMARY

			MONTH TO DATE	YEAR TO DATE
NET MARKET VALUE OF PRICED SECURITIES	16408.50			
NET MONEY BALANCE	.47CR	REAL FUND DIVIDENDS	28.75	206.04
NET PORTFOLIO VALUE	16408.97			
INCLUDED ABOVE ARE MONEY MARKET FUNDS OF	3326.00			
OPENING NET MONEY BALANCE	.26CR			
PURCHASES	1435.54			
SALES	1407.00CR			
INCOME	28.75CR			
CLOSING NET MONEY BALANCE	.47CR			

ACCOUNT ACTIVITY

DATE	TRANSACTION	QUANTITY	DESCRIPTION	AMOUNT	TYPE
			BALANCE FORWARD CASH ACCOUNT	.26CR	1
07/20	DIVIDEND		DIV RECEIVED FROM REAL FUND	28.75CR	1
07/20	BOUGHT	28	REAL FUND A/C OF REINVEST	28.00	1
07/21	BOUGHT	3	CALL 100 CHRYSLER CORP. EXP 10/17/87	1407.54	1
			@ 35.000 A/C OPEN		
			EXECUTED ON CBOE @ 4 1/2		
07/22	SOLD	-1407	REAL FUND @ 1	1407.00CR	1
			CLOSING BALANCE CASH ACCOUNT	0.47CR	1

RECAP LFR MUTUAL FUNDS

TRANSACTION	QUANTITY	DESCRIPTION	AMOUNT
TOTAL BOUGHT	28	REAL FUND	28.00
TOTAL SOLD	-1407	REAL FUND	1407.00CR
TOTAL DIVIDENDS		REAL FUND	28.75CR

SECURITY POSITIONS

TYPE	QUANTITY	DESCRIPTION	PRICE	VALUE	RATE	EST. INCOME
CASH	200	HOLIDAY CORP DELAWARE	32.000	6400.00		
CASH	3326	REAL FUND	1.000	3326.00		
CASH	5000	REGENCY EQUITIES CP	.969	4845.00		
CASH	3	CALL 100 CHRYSLER CORP. EXP 10/17/87	612.500	1837.50		
		@ 35.000				
		**** ACCOUNT TOTAL ****		16408.50		

END OF STATEMENT

SPECIMEN

READING YOUR MUTUAL FUND STATEMENT

Mutual fund statements vary widely. If you have queries about your fund's statement, call its toll-free number. The sample on the right is for Fidelity's High Yield Fund, which invests in bonds. It is sometimes referred to as a junk bond fund. This fund issues quarterly statements. No two statements are alike, but following are some common elements:

The client's social security number is marked "on file." To get information about the account, the social security number must be given.

This account was opened on March 4 with a deposit of $5,000, which bought 501.505 shares at $9.97 per share. The customer has opted to have both dividends and capital gains reinvested, rather than taking cash. Note line at the bottom left.

Once a month the fund reinvests dividend income. Note the purchase of smaller amounts of shares: 3.854 shares on March 31 were purchased at $9.96 per share for a total dollar amount of $38.39. The total of all reinvested dividends is indicated on the bottom line.

The second line from the bottom of the report shows that the current value of the total number of shares held (514.872 shares) is $4,875.84. The customer has lost $124.16 over the 3-month period.

The current yield is not given on the statement. You must call the fund to get this figure for each statement period. Write the yields on your returns as you receive them, or on your record sheet (see page 39).

The statement also does not provide your annual return, the figure you most wish to obtain. You can calculate this yourself:

1. Enter the dollar investment at the beginning of this period. $_____
2. Enter the current market value. $_____
   (If not spelled out on your statement, multiply the number of shares by the current NAV.)
3. Enter the total of any dividends and capital gains received during the period covered by the statement. _____
4. Enter the sum of lines 2 and 3 here. _____
5. Divide the amount on line 4 by the amount on line 1 and enter the result. _____
6. Subtract 1 from the amount on line 5 and multiply the result by 100. This tells you the percentage change during the period covered by the statement. _____%
7. Enter the number of months covered by the statement. _____
8. Enter the result of 12 divided by line 7. _____
9. Enter the result of line 8 multiplied by line 6. _____

DETERMINING YIELD

Since current yield is not given on the statement, you can arrive at a rough estimate this way:

1. Add up the reinvested income for the period covered by the statement (in our sample this would be $38.39 + $45.62 + $45.23 = $129.24).
2. To estimate annual reinvested income, multiply the number from step 1 by the total number of statements you would receive in 12 months: use 4 if you receive quarterly statements, 12 if you get monthly statements (in our sample, 4 × $129.24 = $516.96).
3. Divide the estimate of annual reinvested income from step 2 by the amount of your initial deposit to determine current yield (in our sample, $516.96 ÷ $5,000 = 0.10339 or approximately 10.34%).

YOUR MUTUAL FUND AND TAXES

- *Switching* from one fund to another, even within a family of funds, is a taxable event. Profits accumulated are taxable when rolled over.
- *Dividends* earned by the fund, either paid out or reinvested, are taxed. Municipal bond funds are free of federal taxes unless they contain a new type of taxable bond. Ask your representative.
- *Selling shares* also generates taxes and you are required to figure their original cost, which you can do two ways: (1) by determining that the first shares you bought were the first ones sold, or (2) by identifying the specific purchase date and cost of the shares you're selling. (This second method requires excellent record-keeping on your part.)
- *Buy shares* right after the fund makes its distribution to avoid paying tax on that payout.

EVALUATING YOUR FUND'S PROGRESS

You'll note that the most important item, your total rate of return, may not be spelled out on your statement. Here's what you need to know about any fund's return:

- The NAV (net asset value), which is listed in the paper for the major funds, is seldom an accurate reflection of a fund's performance. The NAV represents only the fund's total assets divided by the number of shares outstanding.
- Yield, too, is often misleading, except of course in those funds set up specifically to generate income. Yield measures dividends per share as a percentage of the offering price, but it does not tell you if the shares have increased or decreased in value.
- *Total return* is the crucial yardstick, since it measures share appreciation, dividends, plus capital gains distribution. If a total return figure is not printed on your statement, call your fund.

For additional suggestions, see IRS booklet #564.

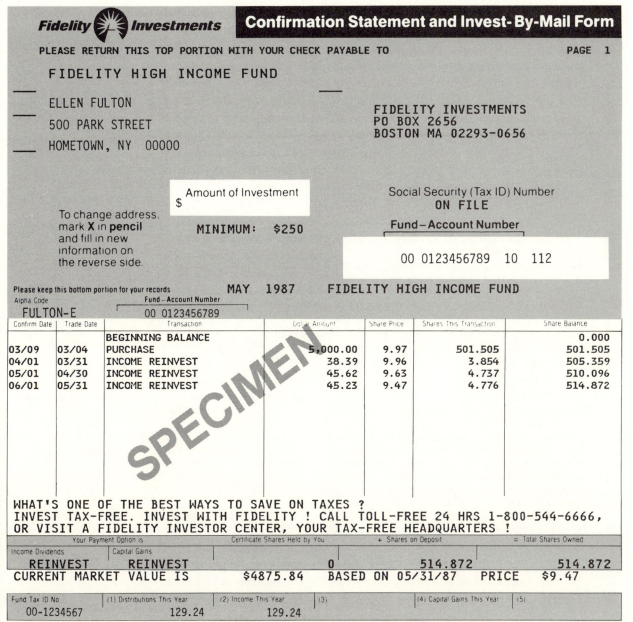

Fidelity Investments — Confirmation Statement and Invest-By-Mail Form

PLEASE RETURN THIS TOP PORTION WITH YOUR CHECK PAYABLE TO PAGE 1

FIDELITY HIGH INCOME FUND

ELLEN FULTON
500 PARK STREET
HOMETOWN, NY 00000

FIDELITY INVESTMENTS
PO BOX 2656
BOSTON MA 02293-0656

Amount of Investment
$

MINIMUM: $250

To change address.
mark **X** in **pencil**
and fill in new
information on
the reverse side.

Social Security (Tax ID) Number
ON FILE

Fund–Account Number

00 0123456789 10 112

Please keep this bottom portion for your records **MAY 1987   FIDELITY HIGH INCOME FUND**

Alpha Code **FULTON-E**   Fund – Account Number   00 0123456789

Confirm Date	Trade Date	Transaction	Dollar Amount	Share Price	Shares This Transaction	Share Balance
		BEGINNING BALANCE				0.000
03/09	03/04	PURCHASE	5,000.00	9.97	501.505	501.505
04/01	03/31	INCOME REINVEST	38.39	9.96	3.854	505.359
05/01	04/30	INCOME REINVEST	45.62	9.63	4.737	510.096
06/01	05/31	INCOME REINVEST	45.23	9.47	4.776	514.872

SPECIMEN

WHAT'S ONE OF THE BEST WAYS TO SAVE ON TAXES ?
INVEST TAX-FREE. INVEST WITH FIDELITY ! CALL TOLL-FREE 24 HRS 1-800-544-6666,
OR VISIT A FIDELITY INVESTOR CENTER, YOUR TAX-FREE HEADQUARTERS !

Your Payment Option is		Certificate Shares Held by You	+ Shares on Deposit	= Total Shares Owned
Income Dividends	Capital Gains			
REINVEST	REINVEST	0	514.872	514.872

CURRENT MARKET VALUE IS $4875.84   BASED ON 05/31/87   PRICE $9.47

Fund Tax ID No	(1) Distributions This Year	(2) Income This Year	(3)	(4) Capital Gains This Year	(5)
00-1234567	129.24	129.24			

Account questions? Customer service open 24 hours. Call toll-free (800) 544-7777.
In Massachusetts and Alaska call collect (617) 227-1888.

READING YOUR CENTRAL ASSET MANAGEMENT ACCOUNT STATEMENT

You can keep all your records in one place—checking, money market account, brokerage account, and mutual fund—by opening a central asset management account. These accounts roll all your investments under one roof and offer check-writing privileges as well as margin accounts and credit or debit cards.

First offered by Merrill Lynch about a decade ago, today they are available from most large brokerage firms, many discount firms, and increasing numbers of banks. Initial requirements for opening tend to be high, usually $10,000 plus annual fees of $50, although less expensive versions exist, so make some phone calls before signing on.

Although these accounts do indeed centralize your investing, they have several disadvantages you should be aware of:

■ With access to more borrowing power than in other types of accounts, you may be tempted to spend more than is wise.

■ A margin loan may be automatically triggered if you don't have enough money in your money market account to cover a transaction.

■ If you receive a debit card rather than a credit card, your account is debited within a few days after purchases are made. With a standard credit card there is a float period of up to 45 days.

READING THE STATEMENT

On the opposite page is a sample statement for the E. F. Hutton Asset Management Account (AMA), which includes a brokerage account, check-writing privileges for any amount through Provident National Bank of Philadelphia, and an American Express Gold Card. In addition, any idle funds are automatically swept into a money market fund. Other options include a fund that invests in government securities or one investing in tax-exempt municipal bonds.

The requirement to open this account is $10,000 in cash or $20,000 in marginable securities or any equivalent combination. The fee is $80 a year, which includes cost of the Gold Card. It is insured by SIPC.

This particular central asset account offers a credit, not a debit, card. AMA clients receive a monthly statement from American Express in addition to their monthly statement from E. F. Hutton. This statement itemizes all Gold Card transactions and includes copies of charge receipts. Unless you decide to pay this bill directly, your AMA account is debited on the date indicated on the American Express statement. E. F. Hutton first uses any cash that has not yet been invested in your money fund to pay American Express. Next,

proceeds from the redemption of money market fund shares are used. Lastly, a loan is made against the securities in your margin account. The firm maintains that this way you never lose unnecessary interest.

The margin account enables you to borrow up to the margin value of the securities in your account by writing a check or using your Gold Card. These loans are made at the brokerage house rate, which is somewhere between 0.75% and 2.25% above the broker's call rate. This could be a potentially dangerous way to borrow. It is not suggested for all investors.

You'll notice that the statement is divided into six sections. *The top section* provides a general summary of what occurred during the month. The client wrote 5 checks worth $2,707.51, paid American Express $1,102.14 for items charged, and deposited $17,677.15 into the account. During the month the money fund earned $320 worth of interest.

Note the section marked Status: Available assets indicates the dollar amount you can write a check for; it is your loan value. Available buying power indicates the amount of additional securities you can buy without having to add more money. Net worth is the dollar amount you would receive if you liquidated the entire account.

The second section itemizes what E. F. Hutton has reported to the IRS for tax purposes, both for the month and for the year to date.

The third section is a chronological listing of all the month's transactions. They are clearly identified by symbols next to the transactions. For example, I = income, B = bought, S = sold, and D = deposit. You can run down this list and find out everything that took place, including purchase and sale of stocks, dividends, and check payments.

Section four summarizes the amount bought this month ($28,990), the amount sold, amount deposited, etc.

Section five provides a rough outline of the checks written. Canceled checks are returned separately by the Provident National Bank.

The sixth section explains what's in the brokerage account—stocks and bonds, etc. The current market price per share of each stock is given, plus the value of the holdings. For instance, this client bought 100 shares of AT&T at $17.25 per share. The total value of his AT&T holdings is $1,725, current dividend yield is 6.96%, and he can expect to receive $120 in dividends for the year. His brokerage account is worth a total of $78,979. Note that this matches the figure in section 1 under Status.

This section also contains the value of the cash fund, which in this case is $39,891.

STATEMENT OF ACCOUNT

Statement Period	Soc. Sec./Tax I.D. #	Account Number	Page

```
JOSEPH N NELSON          06/01/XX-06/30/XX    123 45 6789   A19 12345   1
2063 MT PLEASANT RD
ANYWHERE USA 12345       ACCOUNT EXECUTIVE : JOHN SMITH
                         TELEPHONE : 212-742-5000
                         OFFICE : ONE BATTERY PARK PLAZA
                                  NEW YORK  NY 10004
                         A M A   A C C O U N T
```

AMA HIGHLIGHTS FOR JUNE

ACTIVITY		MONEY FUNDS	OPENING	CLOSING	INCOME	STATUS	
5 CHECKS PAID	2,707.51	HUTTON AMA CASH FUND	30,500	39,891	320.00	AVAILABLE ASSETS	59,435
GOLD CARD PAID	1,102.14					BUYING POWER	39,088
DEPOSITS	17,677.15					PRICED PORTFOLIO	78,979
						NET WORTH	78,979

DISTRIBUTION

	REPORTED TO IRS		NOT REPORTED TO IRS	
	THIS PERIOD	YEAR TO DATE	THIS PERIOD	YEAR TO DATE
DIVIDEND	450.00	4,518.72		

ACCOUNT BALANCES

TYPE	CLOSING	OPENING
CASH	.00	.50CR
MARGIN	.00	.00
TOTAL	.00	.50CR

DATE	TYPE	TRANSACTION	QUANTITY	DESCRIPTION	PRICE	AMOUNT	BALANCE
06 01	2	I-CASH DIVIDEND		TOLEDO EDISON PF3.47		130.00CR	130.50CR
06 04	2	B-BOUGHT	200	HYDRAULIC COMPANY	21	4,306.00-	
	1	S-SOLD TO PAY FOR BUY	4,176-	HUTTON AMA CASH FUND	1	4,176.00	.50CR
06 05	2	D-DEPOSIT		CHECK RECEIVED		17,677.15CR	
	2	P-PAID 2 AMA CHECK(S)				1,100.15-	16,577.50CR
06 06	1	B-BOUGHT	16,577	HUTTON AMA CASH FUND	1	16,577.00-	.50CR
06 15	2	B-BOUGHT	200	HYDRAULIC COMPANY	20	4,204.00-	
	1	S-SOLD TO PAY FOR BUY	4,204-	HUTTON AMA CASH FUND	1	4,204.00	.50CR
06 19	2	P-PAID 3 AMA CHECK(S)				1,607.36-	1,606.86-
06 20	1	S-SOLD ON 06-19 FOR CK/CHG	1,607-	HUTTON AMA CASH FUND	1	1,607.00	.14CR
06 22	2	S-SOLD	100-	GTE CORPORATION	36 5/8	3,583.00CR	3,583.14CR
06 25	1	B-BOUGHT	3,583	HUTTON AMA CASH FUND	1	3,583.00-	.14CR
06 26	1	I-DIVIDEND THRU 06-25		HUTTON AMA CASH FUND		320.00CR	
	1	B-REINVEST AMA A/O 06-25	320	HUTTON AMA CASH FUND	1	320.00-	.14CR
06 29	2	P-PAID		GOLD CARD BILL		1,102.14-	
	1	S-SOLD	1,102-	HUTTON AMA CASH FUND	1	1,102.00CR	.00

TRANSACTION BY CLASS

OPENING BAL(CR)	B-BOUGHT(-)	S-SOLD(CR)	I-INCOME(CR)	D-DEPOSIT(CR)	P-PAID OUT(-)	CLOSING BAL
.50	28,990.00	14,672.00	450.00	17,677.15	3,809.65	.00

AMA CHECKING ACCOUNT TRANSACTIONS

CHECK	DATE	ITEM #..........AMOUNT	CHECK	DATE	ITEM #..........AMOUNT	CHECK	DATE	ITEM #..........AMOUNT
20102	06 05	44867648 995.15	20103	06 05	45358367 105.00	20104	06 19	60007209 268.00
20105	06 19	60332444 974.68	20106	06 19	60353189 364.68			
				5 CHECKS TOTAL	2,707.51		AVAILABLE ASSETS	59,435

YOUR PORTFOLIO

TYPE	QUANTITY	SYMBOL		PRICE	MARKET VALUE	ANNUAL INCOME(EST)	CURRENT YIELD(%)
2	100	* T	AMERICAN TEL AND TEL	17.250	1,725	120	6.96
2	350	* XON	EXXON CORPORATION	40.750	14,263	1,190	8.34
1	39,891		HUTTON AMA CASH FUND	1.000	39,891	4,097	10.27
2	500	THC	HYDRAULIC COMPANY	18.750	9,375	960	10.24
2	100	* IBM	INTL BUS MACHINES	105.750	10,575	440	4.16
2	150	TEDH	TOLEDO EDISON PF3.47	21.000	3,150	521	16.54
* LISTED OPTION AVAILABLE			PORTFOLIO TOTAL		78,979	7,328	9.28

**** ACCOUNT NET WORTH   78,979 ****

CUSTOMER SERVICE CENTER • TOLL FREE • 800-334-4636
E.F. Hutton & Company Inc. • Main Office: One Battery Park Plaza • New York, NY 10004

A DAY IN THE LIFE OF A STOCK

Once you've opened your account, you can place an order by telephone, mail, telex, or, if you've nothing else to do on your lunch break, in person. This fictional example will give you a sense of what takes place. Keep in mind that every firm has different procedures and they may vary slightly from this particular trade.

TUESDAY, 9:10 A.M.

You phone your broker and tell him you'd like to invest in Clorox. He punches in the symbol for Clorox (CLX) on his quote machine and tells you it's bid at 35 and offered at 35¼. This means that 35, the bid, is the highest price any buyer wanted to pay at the time the quote was given on the floor of the Exchange and that 35¼, the asked, was the lowest price any seller would take.

9:16 A.M.

He confirms your opinion that Clorox is a solid company with a history of continual dividend payouts and that it meets your investment objectives. You place a market order (see page 57) for 1,000 shares.

9:30 A.M.

The New York Stock Exchange opens.

9:45 A.M.

Your broker has coffee and danish (a bagel if he's a New York broker) while he fills out an order form, which will include some or all of the following data:
■ Your name ■ Your account number ■ Stock symbol ■ Number of shares ■ Price indication (market, limit, etc.) ■ Broker's name ■ Buy ■ Sell ■ Exchange (NYSE/AMEX/OTC) ■ Type of account (cash/margin) ■ Disposition of securities (transfer to customer, keep in street name, deliver to bank) ■ Sale proceeds (retain/pay out) ■ Settlement date ■ Solicited/unsolicited order

9:50 A.M.

This order is handed to the firm's order clerk who immediately enters it into a computer.

10:05 A.M.

Your order is transmitted by computer to the floor of the New York Stock Exchange where Clorox trades. Your firm's floor broker takes the order because it is sizeable. (A firm's floor broker executes orders on the floor for the firm.) Smaller orders (typically under 1,000 shares) are handled by the new DOT (Direct Order Transfer.)

10:12 A.M.

The floor broker asks the specialist for the market in CLX, at the same time checking the indicator to see where it last traded. It was 35.

10:13 A.M.

The specialist says "35 to ¼."

10:16 A.M.

There are several other bids in at 35 because of active trading, so the broker wants to complete the trade quickly. He bids 35⅛, which he states as "35⅛ for 1,000."

10:17 A.M.

The specialist gives no response, which means the bid is not accepted.

10:18 A.M.

The broker must bid higher: "I'll take 1,000 at ¼."

10:19 A.M.

The specialist says: "Sold!" No papers exchange hands. Both write the details in their books. The honor system is in full force.

10:24 A.M.

The floor broker reports the purchase of 1,000 shares of Clorox by computer back to your brokerage firm. At the same time the transaction is posted to your account, also by computer.

10:25 A.M.

The transaction, which pushed Clorox up by a quarter of a point, is also relayed by computer to the "ticker tape," which is no longer a tape but a computerized system. A few minutes later, further trading boosts CLX to 36 and the "tape" is changed again.

11:30 A.M.

Once the order has been executed, your broker will call you giving the price and settlement date (the day on which securities sold must be delivered or the date on which securities bought must be paid for). If you're an active trader, your broker will ring you as soon as possible.

4:00 P.M.

Otherwise you'll be called at the end of the day or the next morning.

5:00 P.M.

The brokerage firm mails you a confirmation, which details:
■ Name of security ■ Trade rate ■ Execution price ■ Commissions ■ Net amount, including commissions ■ Number of shares (principal amount for bonds) ■ Settlement date ■ Where executed ■ Accrued interest (bonds)

6:30 P.M.

You watch the nightly business news of TV and learn that CLX closed at 37¼, up 2¼ points. Visions of a new swimming pool dance in your head!

WEDNESDAY, 2:30 P.M.

You receive the confirmation and write a check made out to the brokerage firm with your account number on the face of the check. You pay the total amount, including commission, and record the transaction in *Your Year-Round Investment Planner* (page 37).

3:00 P.M. "THE CHECK IS IN THE MAIL!"

You mail the check immediately so payment will reach the firm by settlement day, 5 business days after the trade is executed.

PART FOUR

TAXING ISSUES

The Sixteenth Amendment, passed in 1913, empowered Congress to collect income taxes. The Tax Reform Act of 1986 managed to revolutionize the entire structure, in the process giving more of your investment income to Uncle Sam and less to you.

The so-called reform has forced Americans to view investments in a new light, placing greater emphasis on income and less on tax write-offs. The key changes, against which all investment decisions must be measured, are fairly straightforward:

TAX BRACKETS   Prior to reform there were 15 tax brackets, ranging from 11 to 50%. Now there are essentially two: 15 and 28%, although there's a third bracket of 33% for higher-income earners—individuals earning $43,150 to $89,560 and joint filers earning $71,900 to $149,250.

CAPITAL GAINS   Prior to reform, when you sold a stock, bond, or other asset held 6 months or longer, it was regarded as a long-term capital gain and only 40% of that gain was taxed. Today capital gains are 100% taxed so it no longer matters how long you hold an asset.

IRAs   Prior to reform, the annual $2,000 IRA contribution was tax deductible. That deduction was eliminated for many wage earners.

TAX SHELTERS   Prior to reform, tax shelters, especially limited partnerships, generated deductions that greatly exceeded income. These ''paper'' write-offs can no longer be used to shelter income from wages, interest, dividends, capital gains, or royalties. Such losses, which are considered ''passive'' can only be used to offset income from other passive losses. Therefore, limited partnerships now must be economically sound and generate income to be attractive investments.

TAXABLE EQUIVALENT YIELDS

It is worth investing in taxable vehicles when the return you keep is greater than comparable tax-free yields. Use this chart as a general guide.

FEDERAL TAX BRACKET (1988 AND BEYOND)	TO MATCH A TAX-FREE YIELD OF						
	5%	6%	7%	8%	9%	10%	11%
	YOU MUST EARN THIS YIELD ON A TAXABLE INVESTMENT:						
15%	5.8	7.1	8.2	9.4	10.6	11.9	12.9
28%	6.9	8.3	9.7	11.1	12.5	13.9	15.3
33%	7.5	9.0	10.4	11.9	13.4	14.9	16.4

FEDERAL TAX BRACKETS

Until Congress revises the tax code again, these rates apply beginning in tax year 1988 (taxes due April 15th of the following year).

SINGLE

IF THE TAXABLE INCOME IS:

OVER—	BUT NOT OVER—	YOUR TAX IS—	OF THE AMOUNT OVER—
0	$17,850	. . . . 15%	0
$17,850	43,150	$ 2,677.50 + 28%	$17,850
43,150	89,560	9,761.50 + 33%	43,150
89,560	. . .	25,076.80 + 28% *	89,560

* Surcharge for phaseout of personal exemptions: add a 5% surcharge on income in excess of $89,560, up to an additional tax of $546 per personal exemption.

MARRIED FILING JOINTLY

IF THE TAXABLE INCOME IS:

OVER—	BUT NOT OVER—	YOUR TAX IS—	OF THE AMOUNT OVER—
0	$ 29,750	. . . . 15%	0
$ 29,750	71,900	$ 4,462.50 + 28%	$ 29,750
71,900	149,250	16,264.50 + 33%	71,900
149,250	. . .	41,790.00 + 28% *	149,250

* Surcharge for phaseout of personal exemptions: add a 5% surcharge on income in excess of $149,250, up to an additional tax of $546 per personal exemption.
Source: Dean Witter

ALTERNATIVE MINIMUM TAX

If your income is high you may be subject to the 21% alternative minimum tax (AMT), which is designed to ensure that all taxpayers pay some tax even though they have allowable deductions, exclusions, and credits.

To determine roughly whether you are subject to the AMT, (1) add all preference items to your adjusted gross income; (2) subtract $40,000 if you are married and filing a joint return, $30,000 if single, or $20,000 if married and filing separately; (3) multiply this amount by 21% to arrive at your AMT. If your liability is greater under the AMT than under the regular tax, then you must pay the AMT.

Your accountant will provide you with a list of preference items.

Note: the exemptions (i.e., the $40,000, $30,000, or $20,000) are phased out for high-income taxpayers. The amount is reduced by 25 cents for each $1 that taxable income exceeds $112,000 for individuals and $150,000 for married couples. All passive losses from tax shelters and other investments must be added to taxable income in calculating AMT. Earnings on municipal bonds for nongovernment projects are also subject to AMT.

For more detailed information on the AMT, consult your accountant and see IRS publication #909, "Alternative Minimum Tax."

STATE TAX LIABILITY ON PERSONAL INCOME

Do you know what income tax rate you fit into, at the state level? Are you lucky enough to live in a state without an income tax? Only residents of seven states are. If you live in any of the states listed below or the District of Columbia, Uncle Sam isn't the only one after your income. Your state treasury wants a share as well. To list all of the brackets with all their exceptions would take more pages than the rest of the book. For instance, Minnesota alone has sixteen brackets, and that is just for married people filing joint returns; some states base their rates on federal taxable income, others on taxable net income, and still others on adjusted gross income, not to mention those who divide their tax brackets by dollar amount of earned income. This list gives a broad outline of tax rates across the country. To find the rate in your state applicable to you, contact your state capitol, state treasury, or state legislator's office.

ALABAMA   From 2%, increasing in increments to 5% for over $6,000.

ARIZONA   From 2%, increasing in increments to just under 8% for over $6,930.

ARKANSAS   From 1%, increasing in increments to 7% for over $25,000.

CALIFORNIA   From no tax, increasing in increments to 11% for over $28,790.

COLORADO   Five percent of federal taxable income.

CONNECTICUT   From 1%, increasing in increments to 8.8% for over $40,000.

DELAWARE   From 1%, increasing in increments to 8.8% for over $40,000.

DISTRICT OF COLUMBIA   From 2%, increasing in increments to 11% for over $25,000.

GEORGIA   From 1%, increasing in increments to 6% for over $10,000.

HAWAII   From 2.25%, increasing in increments to 10% for over $40,000.

IDAHO   From 2%, increasing in increments to 8.2% over $20,000.

ILLINOIS   Two and one-half percent of taxable net income.

INDIANA   Three percent of adjusted gross income.

IOWA   From 0.5%, increasing in increments to 13% for over $76,725.

KANSAS   From 2%, increasing in increments to 9% for over $25,000.

KENTUCKY   From 2%, increasing in increments to 6% for over $8,000.

LOUISIANA   From 2%, increasing in increments to 6% for over $50,000.

MAINE   From 1%, increasing in increments to 10% for over $25,000.

MARYLAND   From 2%, increasing in increments to 5% for over $3,000.

MASSACHUSETTS   Five percent on earned income and annuities.

MICHIGAN   Four and six-tenths percent of taxable income.

MINNESOTA   From 1.5%, increasing in increments to 14% for over $32,920.

MISSISSIPPI   From 3%, increasing in increments to 5% for over $10,000.

MISSOURI   From 1.5%, increasing in increments to 6% for over $9,000.

MONTANA   From 2%, increasing in increments to 11% for over $46,400.

NEBRASKA   From 2%, increasing in increments to 5.9% for over $45,000.

NEW HAMPSHIRE   Five percent of income.

NEW JERSEY   From 2%, increasing in increments to 3.5% for over $50,000.

NEW MEXICO   From 1.8%, increasing in increments to 8.5% for over $41,600.

NEW YORK   From 2%, increasing in increments to 8.75% for over $23,300.

NORTH CAROLINA   From 3%, increasing in increments to 7% for over $10,000.

NORTH DAKOTA   From 2.6%, increasing in increments to 12% for over $50,000.

OHIO   From 0.751%, increasing in increments to 6.9% for over $100,000.

OKLAHOMA   From 0.5%, increasing in increments to 6% for over $15,000.

OREGON   From 5%, increasing in increments to 9% for over $10,000.

PENNSYLVANIA   Two and one-tenth percent of some taxable income.

RHODE ISLAND   Twenty-three and forty-six percent of modified federal income tax.

SOUTH CAROLINA   From no tax, increasing in increments to 7% for over $13,600.

TENNESSEE   Six percent of income.

UTAH   From 2.25%, increasing in increments to 7.75% for over $7,500.

VERMONT   Twenty-five and eight-tenths percent of federal income tax.

VIRGINIA   From 2%, increasing in increments to 5.75% for over $14,000.

WEST VIRGINIA   From 3%, increasing in increments to 6.5% for over $60,000.

WISCONSIN   From 5%, increasing in increments to 7.9% for over $40,000.

TAX CHECKLIST

The following tax tips will help you cut taxes and hold onto more of your income. Some ideas are based on the new law; others are old standbys that still work. Check with your accountant before implementing these or any other tax savers, as individual circumstances vary.

- *Look for high-yielding stocks, bonds, and other investments,* since the drop in tax rates may mean you can keep more of your income. *Ideas:* (1) Investigate public utility companies, REITs, limited partnerships, closed-end bond funds, and junk bond mutual funds. (2) Sign up for dividend reinvestment plans. (3) Use T-bills for income and to defer taxes.

- *Give to your parents.* You can claim a $1,900 dependency exemption for each parent you support—that's an increase over $1,080.

- *Buy mutual fund shares after the fund's annual capitalization payout,* usually in January. If you buy just before a fund makes its distribution, these gains are included in the price and you will be taxed on gains you did not receive. Call the fund to get distribution data.

- *Use life insurance to benefit heirs.* The death benefit passes to your beneficiary free of income tax if it's under $600,000. (IRA earnings are taxable to heirs at their income tax rate.)

- *Hire your spouse* so he or she will be eligible to invest $2,000 in an IRA. Be sure to pay the going rate and keep accurate records.

- *If you have self-employment income, open a Keogh plan.* All contributions are tax deductible. You can contribute up to 20% of your self-employment income or $30,000, whichever is less.

- *If you are self-employed, purchase health insurance.* Until 1989, you can deduct 25% of the premiums.

- *If you're in a state with high income taxes, buy triple-exempt* municipal bonds, bond funds, or unit investment trusts.

- *Pay your bills on time.* Deductions for personal interest on credit cards, auto, and personal loans are being phased out.

- *Give your children investments that won't be taxed until they turn 14;* then the income is taxed at their presumably lower rate. Until they are 14, unearned income in excess of $1,000 is taxed at the parent's rate. *Ideas:* EE savings bonds, CDs, zero coupon municipal bonds, tax-exempt mutual funds.

- *Shift income by hiring your children*—but only at reasonable rates. Their earnings will be taxed at their lower rate, and it's tax-free up to $3,000. You can deduct their wages as a business expense.

- *Get a tax credit of 10 or 20% for investing in a certified historic rehabilitation project;* ask your stockbroker. Tax credits (vs tax deductions) reduce your taxes dollar for dollar.

- *If your income is under $100,000, investigate rental real estate.* Even if you have no passive income, you can write off $25,000 of losses from rental real estate. Reduced write-offs are available for those with adjusted gross incomes between $100,000 and $150,000.

- *Shelter your savings.* The tax advantage of life insurance (tax-deferred buildup of cash value within the policy) was preserved. And unlike IRAs and Keoghs, there's no dollar cap on your investment. *Ideas:* annuities, insurance, taxed-deferred savings plan at work, single premium whole life.

- *Give your children tax-free money.* Parents together can give up to $20,000 a year to each child free of taxes. Set up a Uniform Gift to Minors Act custodial account with your broker.

- *If you have a margin account,* the interest you pay is deductible only to the extent that it is offset by investment income from dividends, capital gains, and limited partnerships. To deduct $500 worth of interest on a margin loan, you must report at least $500 of investment income on your IRS 1040 Form.

- *Reduce taxes by investing in a 401(k) plan;* maximum is $7,000 a year or 25% of your salary, whichever is less. Earnings grow tax-deferred.

- *Swap property.* Ask your accountant about swapping property instead of selling it, to postpone paying taxes on your capital gains until you sell for real cash. (*Note:* Some states levy a tax on swaps.) Applies to property held for business or investment purposes; not your home, except for the rental portion if there is one.

- *Buy EE savings bonds for your children.* Neither you nor your child has to pay tax on these bonds until they are converted into cash. So time EE bonds to come due when your child turns 14. Then they will be taxed at the child's lower rate.

- *Purchase a life insurance policy in your child's name.* Single premium life insurance builds up cash value over the years. Earnings are tax-exempt until your child cashes in the policy. If it is cashed in at age 14, all income will be taxed at the child's lower rate. In addition, your child can borrow free of taxes against the interest earned. (See Annuities, page 50.)

- *Set up an irrevocable trust for your child* so that the child will receive less than the $1,000 annual limit until the age of 14. Determine with your accountant when the trust will distribute income. Ideally it should be when your child reaches 14.

PART FIVE

RETIREMENT PLANNING

Whether you dream of sitting on a beach, playing bridge, beginning a new career, or embracing volunteer work, you want those retirement years to be free of money worries. So, whether you're 22, 52, or 62, *make a plan;* if you have one, *reevaluate it.* The new IRS rules regarding corporate plans, pensions, and retirement accounts could make the difference between retirement years that are painful or joyous.

Don't overlook the possibility of getting expert advice on what to do. This is a complicated area, the solutions tricky and complex, and the end results vital. Start with your local social security office. Here you can find out how to apply for benefits, how much you are likely to receive, and what will happen if you retire early. In addition, talk with the personnel officer where you work, attend professionally run seminars on retirement, and look into the benefits of the American Association of Retired Persons. You may also want to consult a professional planner who specializes in retirement. Leave no stone unturned.

On the following pages, you'll find the facts about company pension plans, 401(k)s, IRAs, Keoghs, SEPs, and the old standby, social security.

YOUR RETIREMENT OPTIONS—COMPANY PENSION PLANS

Your company probably has more than one pension or savings plan option for its employees. Yet few of us ever remember the details, or at least not until we start closing in on retirement. Take time this year to study your company's plans so you can make intelligent decisions about future investments.

Begin by drawing up a list of questions; then seek the answers in your employee handbook. If the material is not clear, make an appointment to talk with the personnel department benefits officer; write down the answers as you receive them. Then review your entire retirement strategy to see if you will indeed have enough money for retirement.

soon you will be vested and when you are entitled to a full pension.

2   Your employee-benefit statement, which shows your accrued benefits plus estimates of what you will be paid after retirement.

3   Your employer's Form 5500, which is a statement of the plan's assets and liabilities. An accountant will be able to tell you if the plan is underfunded, and how well it is invested.

For additional help, send $3 to: Pension Rights Center, 1701 K Street, NW, Washington, DC 20006 for a copy of "A Guide to Understanding Your Pension Plan." It explains precisely how benefits are calculated.

QUESTIONS TO ASK ABOUT YOUR PENSION PLAN

- At what age can I get my pension?
- How much will I receive?
- How much less will it be if I retire early?
- What will happen to it if I die?
- How is the plan financed; how solid is it?
- What if I leave the company and then return?
- Can I withdraw money prior to retirement?
- Must I contribute?
- How long must I be employed before I'm fully vested?
- If I leave this job before I'm fully vested, do I retain any portion of my pension? Can I transfer my pension to my new employer?

PENSION-ESE

Conduit IRA: A special type of IRA designed for funds rolled over from a pension payout. Funds can remain in the IRA without incurring a tax penalty until you've set up a Keogh for them.

Forward averaging: Used with a lump sum payment from a pension or Keogh plan, averaging allows you to handle the money as if you had received it over a 5-year period, thus reducing your taxes on it.

Rollover: Transferring money from one tax-deferred account to another in such a way as to preserve the tax-deferred aspects of the investment.

Vested: When an employee receives the right to pension or other benefits contributed by an employer. Vesting occurs after a stated number of years.

You can find out some things from documents that your employer is legally bound to give you. These include:

1   A summary of the plan, which must tell you how

YOUR RETIREMENT OPTIONS—401(k) PLANS

This type of retirement savings plan, also known as a salary reduction plan, allows workers to contribute to a special investment account with their employers matching some or even all of their contributions. The contributions you make are on a pretax basis. The maximum you can contribute is 25% of your yearly compensation or $7,000 a year, whichever is less. *Note:* Because the amount contributed to a 401(k) plan reduces your salary, your federal income tax bill is also reduced. This is a tremendous advantage, so if you are unable

to contribute to your company's plan, you might want to borrow to do so.

Companies that offer 401(k)s all have their own designs, but there are essentially three standard forms: (1) *A pretax thrift plan* in which employers match employees' contributions. The amount is typically 6%. (2) *A salary reduction savings plan* in which the employer does not match your contribution, which is typically 10%. (3) *A cash-deferred profit-sharing plan* in which the employer matches some of your contribution.

You can take your employer's contribution in cash if you like, although it is then taxed at ordinary income rates.

In a 401(k) you will be presented with several investment choices, typically the company's stock, a stock mutual fund, a long-term bond fund, and a money market fund. (Read about each of these choices elsewhere in this book.) In most plans you do not need to stay with the same type of investment the entire time, and in fact, as you get closer to retirement, you will undoubtedly want to switch into more conservative investments.

BORROWING FROM YOUR 401(k)

Not all plans allow you to borrow, and those that do may ask for proof of hardship. But in any case, know the rules before you borrow, otherwise you may find your loan subject to ordinary income taxes. Find out what the interest rate is and the time limit. Most such loans cannot run longer than 5 years unless the money is being used to buy your principal residence (not your vacation home!). The loan, when added to other loans you have taken out elsewhere, cannot be more than $50,000 or 50% of your accrued benefit in the plan, whichever is less. However, you can borrow up to $10,000 even if that's over the accrued benefit benchmark.

DISTRIBUTIONS

You can take your money out either in a lump sum or as an annuity. Under the annuity arrangement, the amount is taxed as ordinary income the year you receive it. In a lump sum arrangement, you can reduce or defer taxes by using averaging, rolling it over into an IRA within 60 days, or transferring it into another qualified plan if you have changed jobs.

YOUR RETIREMENT OPTIONS—IRAs

Using formulas to calculate how much money you will need when you retire is a favorite pastime of insurance experts, actuarial buffs, and financial planners. No one ever agrees and no one really knows. The only thing that's safe to assume is that you'll need as much as possible, or, as Henny Youngman put it, "I've got all the money I'll ever need—if I die by 4 o'clock!"

In recent years, IRAs have been the most popular way to supplement social security benefits, but the 1986 Tax Reform Act made some sharp changes relating to the funding of IRAs.

THE NEW RULES

Prior to tax reform, your annual $2,000 contribution was tax deductible, but this is no longer the case for everyone. If you are covered by a retirement plan at work or a Keogh plan *and* if you have a gross income of over $35,000 ($50,000 for a joint return), you can contribute but it is *not* deductible. Even if you're not covered by an employer plan but your spouse is, or if you're covered by a plan but not yet vested, you're simply out of luck.

The $2,000 tax deduction is available under certain circumstances for married couples with gross incomes of less than $40,000 ($25,000 for singles) even if covered by an employer retirement plan. Above these limits the amount that's deductible declines: $200 for each $1,000 in income until the cutoff point is reached.

If you don't qualify for the deduction but you decide to continue contributing, all earnings will grow tax-free until withdrawn, as in the past. The big question you need to answer is: does the benefit of accumulating earnings tax-free outweigh the drawback of not being able to tap your money prior to age 59½ without a 10% penalty. If you think you might need the money before that age, then without the $2,000 deductibility feature you are probably better off investing elsewhere. An IRA is no longer an investment must for every American.

For example, if you invest $2,000 today at 8%, at the end of 20 years you'll have approximately $9,300. If the taxes due each year on the interest income are 28%, your account would be worth just $6,100 or about $\frac{1}{3}$ less.

REMAINING BENEFITS

IRAs should not causally be tossed out the window without serious consideration, however. An IRA is still a place where earnings can grow tax-deferred, and it's a relatively painless way to save money, especially since you are not required to pay the $2,000 all at once.

In fact, you have 15 months in which to fund your IRA: you can start on January 1 and pay in small amounts until April 15 of the *following* year. (The sooner you begin putting money in, the more it will earn; mark your investment calendar.)

An IRA is also a valuable vehicle for anyone receiving lump sum payouts from company pension or profit-sharing plans, especially since 10-year forward averaging was cut back to 5 by the 1986 reform. In the past, you figured your taxes on these distributions as though you had been paid over a period of 10 years and not all at once. (Those who were age 50 or older on January 1, 1986, still qualify for 10-year averaging.) This means the IRA will grow in importance as a place to make a tax-free rollover of company pension and profit-sharing monies.

FACTS YOU SHOULD KNOW

- *You can open an IRA* if you are under age 70½ and have earned income from such sources as wages, salary, tips, commissions, alimony, self-employment, or bonuses. However, if the only income you have is not earned, such as interest income, dividends, rental income, or pension plan payments, you do not qualify.

- *You can contribute $2,000 a year.* If one spouse is employed and the other is not, you can contribute $2,250 to a spousal IRA. If both you and your spouse have earned income you can have two separate IRAs and each can contribute $2,000 a year. If you and your ex-spouse had a spousal IRA and you are now divorced *and* receiving alimony, you can continue contributing $2,000 a year. Alimony is regarded as earned compensation. There is no minimum amount required to open an IRA, although most trustees insist on $250 or $500.

- *You can invest your IRA in numerous institutions,* but it must be done through a trustee, such as a bank, mutual fund family, brokerage firm, or insurance company. There is no limit on the number of different IRAs you can set up, although each one charges a small fee, which should be taken into consideration: the more trustees, the more expensive.

- *Among the many investments you can use* are stocks, bonds, mutual funds, real estate, U.S. Gold Eagle coins, CDs, and annuities. You may not invest in precious metals, with the exception of the Gold Eagle. Investing in municipal bonds and municipal bond funds or trusts is a waste: These pay lower yields than taxable bonds because they are exempt from federal income tax. You don't need this tax-free benefit since *all* earnings in an IRA grow tax-free until withdrawn. As you read about the leading investment choices in this book, consider using them for your IRA account.

- *If you need to tap your IRA before age 59½,* you can do so temporarily without incurring a penalty through a 60-day rollover. This can be done once every 12 months. When you do, the trustee of your account will file a notification with the IRS. You may also roll over IRA funds in order to change trustees, say from your brokerage firm to a mutual fund. In this situation, you never actually touch the money; it is transferred from one institution to another electronically. If you wish to change trustees, plan well in advance. You'll discover that trustees seldom shift into high gear to facilitate moving your money elsewhere. Any other early withdrawals cause a 10% tax penalty unless you are disabled, in which case you can withdraw all IRA money without a penalty, although you will have to pay income tax on the amount withdrawn.

- *You must begin withdrawing money* in the year following the year you turn 70½. On that date you must also cease making contributions.

ALTERNATIVES TO AN IRA

Without their deductibility factor, IRAs have lost their premier position as a means of building up retirement dollars. Investors should carefully consider alternatives, either to supplement an IRA or to replace it.

Annuities (see page 50) offer the same tax-deferred growth of principal as an IRA but have an added advantage: there's no dollar limit on the amount you can invest. Annuities often have hidden costs, however, which are seldom a feature of the traditional IRA. Some have annual fees, back-end loads, 10% early withdrawal penalties, etc. So shop with care.

Single premium whole life (see page 52) is also a logical alternative, as long as you're disciplined enough not to borrow too much of the principal or pull out too soon.

A SPECIAL NOTE OF CAUTION

If you accidentally contribute more than $2,000 to your IRA in any one year, and if you discover your mistake before you file your taxes for that year, take out the extra money immediately. If you leave that money in your account, thinking the IRS will never notice, think again. It's subject to a 6% penalty—*for every year it stays there.* Then, if you try to take it out, any interest that's been earned will be taxed twice: once as regular income and once because of the 10% early withdrawal penalty.

YOUR RETIREMENT OPTIONS—KEOGHs AND SEPs

Keogh plans fortunately emerged relatively unscathed by tax reform. So if you are self-employed, whether full time or part time, or even if you work full time for someone else, you can have a Keogh, one of the best of the tax-sheltered plans.

In a Keogh plan you can save up to 20% of your net self-employment income or $30,000, whichever is less. (In an IRA, you recall, the limit is $2,000 a year; $2,250 for couples where only one is employed.) You can even have a Keogh if you already have an IRA. Your money compounds tax-free until withdrawn.

You can open your Keogh at a brokerage firm, bank, insurance company, or mutual fund. And you can have as many as you like as long as the combined dollar totals are not over the limit. There is no minimum, but most institutions ask for $250 or more. Fees for opening and managing a Keogh range from zero to about $25.

There are several types of Keoghs and you may want to consult your accountant before deciding which one is best for you.

- *Defined-contribution plans* are the easiest Keogh to set up because the annual payment is a fixed amount. (It takes its name from the fact that the amount you contribute is determined in advance.) Within this category there are two types of Keoghs: a money purchase plan and a profit-sharing plan.

  In the *money purchase plan* you must contribute the same minimum percentage every year unless your business registers a loss. If you underfund your plan you will be fined 5% of the amount underfunded. You have 90 days in which to make up the shortfall; after that you will be fined 100% of the amount.

  If this is too stringent for you, you may want the more flexible *profit-sharing plan*. Here you contribute $30,000 or 13% of your income, whichever is less. You can select a different percentage each year, depending upon how well your company is doing.

- *Defined-benefit plans* offer even greater shelter possibilities because you can deduct whatever you need to contribute in order to achieve an annual retirement income equal to the average of your highest annual earnings over 3 consecutive years. In other words, you establish that monthly retirement amount and then contribute whatever amount is necessary to fund that benefit. To make the proper calculations you must use actuarial figures and submit a form every year to the IRS in which an actuary certifies that the amounts are correct. Expect to pay anywhere from $500 to $15,000 to set up this type of plan, plus additional fees for the annual certification. This plan is de-

signed for the wealthy and/or those close to retirement. The greatest annual benefit you can receive is $90,000 and of course the older you are the more you will have to contribute each year to build up your account so you receive the $90,000 payment.

Regardless of the type of Keogh you select, you can add even more to your retirement earnings by making special nondeductible contributions—up to 6% of your self-employment income after you subtract your deductible Keogh contribution from that income amount. Even though they're not deductible, once they're inside your Keogh they will compound on a tax-deferred basis. You are allowed to withdraw the principal (but not the interest) of your nondeductible contributions whenever you like. In this way, your Keogh is actually a type of tax-sheltered savings account.

EMPLOYEES AND KEOGHS   If you have a Keogh, then so must the people who work for you who are 21 or older or who have worked for you for 3 years. Therefore, if you have employees, make certain you want to undertake the financial commitment of a Keogh.

FORMS TO FILE   A Keogh involves quite a lot of paperwork. The IRS requires you to file disclosure forms every year, and if your Keogh has more than one participant, then you must file IRS Form 5500-C, a complex five-page form. The deadline is July 31 for this form unless your are on your own fiscal year in which case it is the last day of the seventh month of your fiscal year. You can either handle this paperwork yourself or hire an accountant. But it must be done: penalty for filing late is $25 a day up to $15,000.

Form 5500-C must be filed in the first year and then every third year afterwards. During the interim years you must file a shorter form, 5500-R. If there's only you, then you file only Form 5500-R.

TAKING OUT YOUR MONEY

You can begin taking out your Keogh dollars at age 59½; if you do so earlier, you'll be penalized 10% on the amount withdrawn, unless you are disabled. If you borrow from your Keogh you will be taxed 5% on the amount borrowed; you must repay the money in 90 days or there's a 100% penalty.

Withdrawals must begin by April 1 of the year after you turn 70½, even if you are still working. The minimum withdrawal amount is determined by your life expectancy.

There are various ways to withdraw funds, so review them carefully with a tax accountant. Essentially your choices are either to take out the entire amount in a lump sum or receive periodic payments.

You can recalculate your life expectancy each year if you want to reduce the dollar amount of your required withdrawals. You can also reduce them by averaging your life expectancy with that of a spouse who is younger, or even with a beneficiary who is not your spouse.

If you elect to take your Keogh money in a lump sum, you can cut your tax bill by using 5-year forward averaging. (You must have had a Keogh 5 years to qualify.) Then you are taxed as if you had received this money over a 5-year period, thus paying less tax than if you reported the total as ordinary income all in one year. *Note:* After you turn 59½, you can use 5-year forward averaging only once—so if you use it for your pension plan distribution, then you cannot use it with your Keogh. You can get around this restriction: roll over your pension payout into an IRA.

SIMPLIFIED EMPLOYEE PENSION (SEP)

If the paperwork involved in setting up a Keogh plan seems a bit overwhelming, then look into a SEP, or simplified employee pension. It's basically an IRA with higher limits.

In a SEP you can contribute 13% of your self-employment income or $30,000, whichever is less. SEPs can be opened with the same institutions that handle IRAs and Keoghs. In fact, most institutions use the same application form for both a SEP and an IRA, so be certain to designate which you want.

As with IRAs and Keoghs, you can invest in stocks, bonds, mutual funds, etc.; you can begin withdrawing your money at age 59½; and you must start at age 70½.

YOUR RETIREMENT OPTIONS—SOCIAL SECURITY

Social security remains the major source of retirement funds, despite much ballyhooing about whether it will last as long as we do. Although it by no means provides enough to live on, nor is it intended to, payments should be factored into your planning. In most cases you must work 10 years before you receive benefits, although the rules are numerous and complex. Take time now to investigate what is recorded in your name, whether the amounts are accurate, and what you can expect to receive when you retire.

You can determine your possible benefits at any time by using the tables in the brochure "Estimating Your Social Security Benefits," available from your local social security office. Remember, benefits automatically rise after a year in which inflation increases by at least 3%. Full benefits start at age 65; partial benefits at age 62. The later you retire, the better: the government adds 3% for each year you delay taking full benefits for ages 65–70.

Before you reach 60, request Form 7004, "Request for Statement of Earnings." Fill it out and return it. The government will send you an estimate of forthcoming benefits. Do this every three years, because social security statements are explicit only for the last three years; all previous earnings are lumped together. Compare these figures with the earnings reported on your tax return. Report discrepancies.

Three months prior to retirement notify your social security office. Your checks will not be sent automatically when you stop work. You may need to show your birth certificate, marriage license, and/or divorce papers, as well as copies of your W-2 tax withholding statements for the last two years you worked.

WHAT YOU NEED TO RECORD ABOUT YOUR RETIREMENT PLAN

If you have worked for more than one employer and are vested in more than one plan be sure to keep separate records for each plan. The same is true for individuals who have established more than one IRA. Among the facts you should make note of are these:

- Trustee's name, address, phone number
- Company's name, address, phone number
- Account number
- Federal filing number, if any
- Date plan was started

- Date when you were/will be vested
- Your annual contribution
- Employer's annual contribution
- Total amount in plan
- Annual yield
- Type of investment selected: fixed, variable, mutual fund, stocks, CD, bonds
- Withdrawal penalty
- Distribution options: lump sum, annuity (installment), rollover to IRA

PART SIX

YOUR FINANCIAL CALENDAR

In this section you will find 12 blank calendar pages. Make copies for future years and then fill in the dates for the current year. Use these pages to keep track of the important financial dates in your life, such as when to:

- File your estimated taxes
- Make your IRA or Keogh contributions
- Collect or roll over your CD
- Pay insurance premiums
- Review your portfolio with your broker
- Attend meetings of your investment club
- Watch out for triple-witching days

Monthly guidelines are given on pages 82–83 to help you get started. You might also want to record additional information such as the Dow Jones Industrial Average and S&P 500 Index at the beginning of each month. This will make you aware of the market's overall trend. You can add other statistics to your monthly alert: 6-month T-bill rates, the dollar vs the pound, the GNP, etc. Then, once you've organized your financial file and activated your calendar, you'll never again miss an important date, pay a late penalty, or forget about an investment.

PROGRAM TRADING

Mark your calendars! Four times a year, three investments expire on the same day: stock index futures, stock options, and index options. Called the triple-witching days, they are the third Fridays of March, June, September, and December. The big action takes place late in the afternoon when program traders, who must be out of their positions by 4:00, either dump or buy millions of dollars worth of stock. Consequently, the market has huge gains or losses—it's hard for anyone to predict which will happen.

Many Wall Street soothsayers say that program trading is the culprit of such huge price swings. Whether it is or not, you should be aware of its impact because it's going to increase, not decrease, as Wall Street becomes more tightly wedded to the computer.

Program trading is a strategy used by pension funds and other large institutional investors in which computers automatically set off enormous buy and sell orders. The pros use computers to monitor the difference between stock index futures, such as the S&P 500, and the actual market values of the stocks that make up the index. This involves buying or selling what is called a basket or group of stocks that mirror the index. A basket contains hundreds of different stocks worth millions of dollars. When either the basket or the index sells at a sufficient discount or premium in comparison to the other, the program trader locks in a profit by buying one and selling the other.

Program trading decisions have nothing to do with a company's earnings or fundamental strengths; instead, buy and sell decisions are triggered by price discrepancies between the stock market and the index futures market.

For example, if the futures index is trading at a discount to the actual cash index, the arbitrageurs will buy futures and sell stocks. So whenever the price spread between an index, such as the S&P 500, falls below the market value of the underlying stocks, computers automatically begin selling large quantities of stocks. Very often huge price declines as well as a sense of panic result.

On the other hand, if the stock prices of the S&P 500 are way behind the futures, the computers trigger orders to buy these stocks and sell the futures, which can send prices way up.

What can you do? Avoid buying or selling on these days, take a long weekend, and keep your sanity.

CALENDAR GUIDELINES

JANUARY

- Begin gathering your W-2 Forms from each employer.
- Begin collecting Form 1099s from your bank and broker.
- Get out last year's tax return; review it with your accountant.
- The fourth quarterly installment of previous year's estimated income tax is due on the 15th.
- Buy new edition of *Dun & Bradstreet's Guide to $Your Investments$*.

FEBRUARY

- Call any banks, brokerage firms, or employers that have not sent you their IRS forms.
- Estimate your taxable income to determine if you're eligible for an IRA deduction.
- Fund a new IRA to get as much tax-deferred income as possible.
- File appropriate forms for any household help you hired (940, 941, 942). Pay their required social security taxes.
- Visit your local IRS office for copies of free booklets on preparing your taxes.

MARCH

- If you own a business that's taxed as an S corporation, file Form 2553.
- If you are entitled to a lump sum pension distribution, arrange for a rollover to avoid penalty.
- Prepare a rough outline of your taxes.
- Meet with your accountant to review your tax situation.
- Third Friday is triple-witching day.

APRIL

- The 15th is the last day you can mail your tax return.
- The 15th is the last day you can fund your IRA for prior year.

- The 15th is the last day you can file for a 4-month extension of income tax filing.
- The first quarterly installment of estimated taxes for this year is due on the 15th.
- File quarterly tax returns for household help and pay their social security taxes.

MAY

- Review portfolio with broker.
- Start holiday club contribution.
- Pay real estate taxes.

JUNE

- The second quarterly installment of estimated taxes is due on the 15th.
- Third Friday is triple-witching day.

JULY

- Social security taxes due for household help.

AUGUST

- If you received an extension, your tax return is due to avoid penalty.

SEPTEMBER

- The third quarterly installment of estimated tax is due on the 15th.
- Third Friday is triple-witching day.

OCTOBER

- Meet with accountant. Review year's earnings and income to see if you'll be hit with the alternative minimum tax (AMT). If so, discuss ways to lessen impact with both accountant and stockbroker.

NOVEMBER

- Talk to your broker about year-end tax swaps.
- Pay social security taxes for household help and file appropriate forms.

DECEMBER

- If you need to defer income, select appropriate investments with your broker.
- Give up to $10,000 to each child free of gift tax ($20,000 if you're married).
- Set up Keogh account.
- Third Friday is triple-witching day.

USING YOUR FINANCIAL CALENDAR

Here is how one knowledgeable investor makes use of the calendar pages. Make notes about important financial dates beside each page as helpful reminders.

MONTH: _MARCH_

1	2	3	4	5	6	7
Deposit $ in savings-money mkt. account						
8	**9** 8pm Investment Club meets at Ray's	**10**	**11**	**12** Lunch with Broker	**13** IRA contrib. due	**14**
15 CD at Bank of NY comes due	**16**	**17**	**18**	**19**	**20** Triple-Witching Day!	**21**
22	**23**	**24**	**25**	**26**	**27**	**28**
29	**30**	**31** File est. taxes				

REMINDERS

* Read "Heard on the Street" WSJ column on Fridays
* Decide whether to roll over CD at bank
* Review auto insurance; premium due next month
* Find out performance of S&P 500 before lunch with broker
* List topics to discuss with broker ... time for gold? Portfolio performance

MONTH: _____

REMINDERS

MONTH: _____

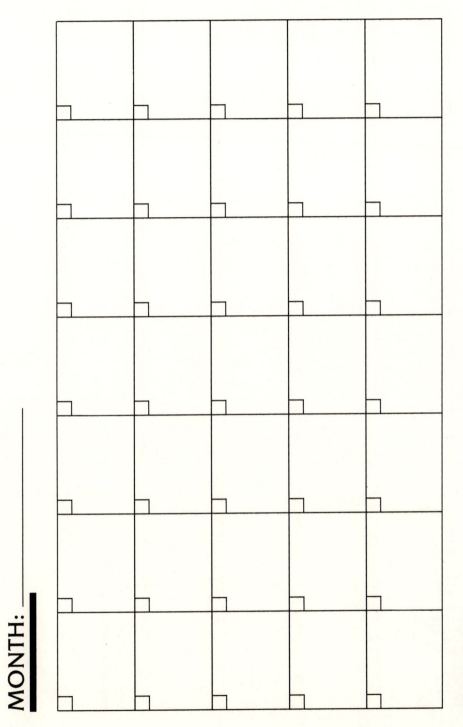

REMINDERS

MONTH: _____

REMINDERS

MONTH: _____

REMINDERS

MONTH: _____

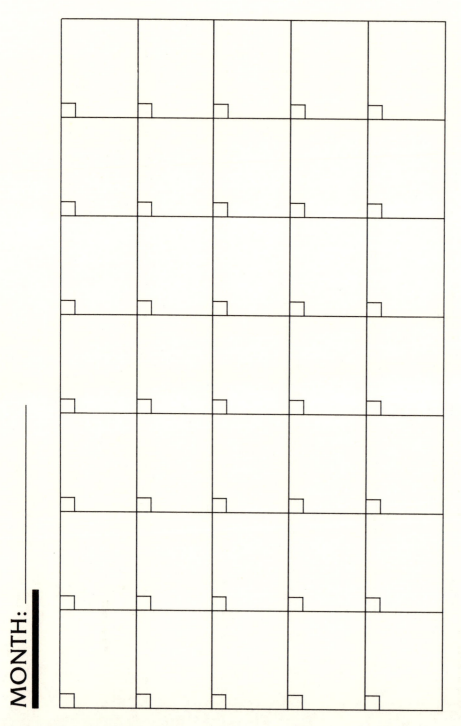

REMINDERS

MONTH: _____

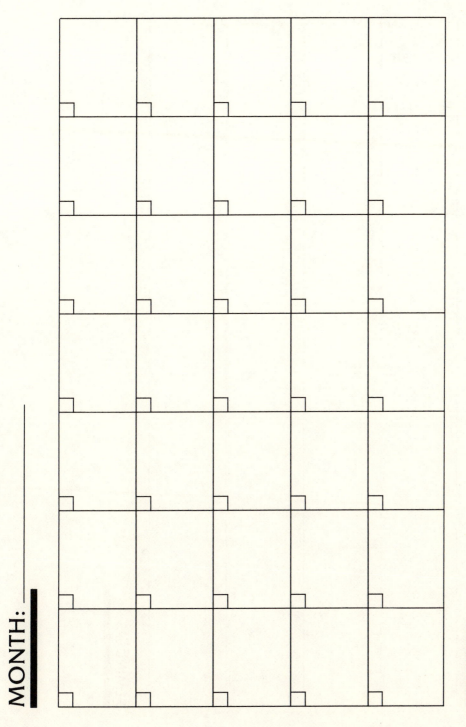

REMINDERS

MONTH: _____

REMINDERS

MONTH: _____

REMINDERS

MONTH: _____

REMINDERS

MONTH: _____

REMINDERS

MONTH: _____

REMINDERS

Dear Reader,

Well, now you have no excuses left. You know the pros and cons, the pluses and minuses, of the top investment vehicles, how to evaluate each one, and the tax consequences involved. And, of course, you have a nice notebook in which to keep track of them. The blank spaces are all there, waiting for you to fill them in. Please do . . . you'll find it comforting as well as useful to know exactly where your money is at all times.

Review your record book on a continual basis—as the economic climate changes, as your personal life evolves, as you grow and prosper. If you spend just two hours each month keeping your book up-to-date, you will always have an instant, accurate picture of your financial status, for you as well as for your accountant, your broker, and Uncle Sam.

I hope you have as much pleasure in tracking your riches as I have had in writing about them.

Nancy Dunnan